CASE STUDIES IN

CULTURAL ANTHROPOLOGY

GENERAL EDITORS

George and Louise Spindler

STANFORD UNIVERSITY

———————

GOPALPUR

A South Indian Village

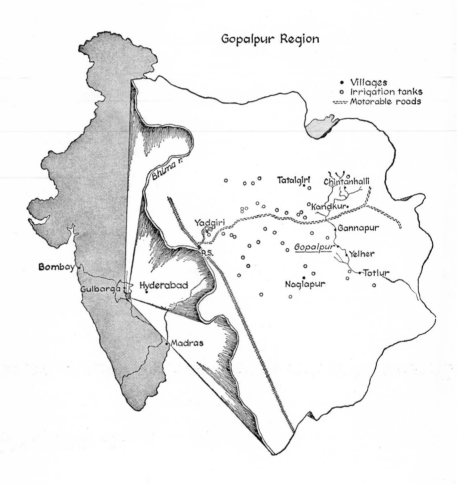

Gopalpur Region

• Villages
○ Irrigation tanks
〰〰 Motorable roads

Bhima r.

Tatalgiri Chintanhalli

Kandkur

Yadgiri

Gannapur

R.S.

Gopalpur

Yelher

Totlur

Naglapur

Bombay

Gulbarga

Hyderabad

Madras

GOPALPUR

A South Indian Village

BY

ALAN R. BEALS

Stanford University

HOLT, RINEHART AND WINSTON

NEW YORK   CHICAGO   SAN FRANCISCO   TORONTO   LONDON

About the Series

THESE CASE studies in cultural anthropology are designed to bring to students, in beginning and intermediate courses in the social sciences, insights into the richness and complexity of human life, as it is lived in different ways and in different places. They are written by men and women who have lived in the societies they write about, and who are professionally trained as observers and interpreters of human behavior. The authors are also teachers, and in writing their books they have kept the students who will read them foremost in their minds. It is our belief that when an understanding of ways of life very different from one's own is gained, abstractions and generalizations about social structure, cultural values, subsistence techniques, and the other universal categories of human social behavior become meaningful.

About the Author

Alan R. Beals, now an assistant professor of anthropology at Stanford University, received his Ph.D. from the University of California in 1954. He has completed field studies of an agricultural community in Northern California (1950); an Air Force bomber crew (1952); and several villages in Southern India (1952-53, 1958-60). He is coauthor with Thomas McCorkle of *Lost Lake*, and has collaborated with John Hitchcock to write a guide for fieldworkers in India. Several of his articles dealing with villages in India have been published in scholarly journals. He is currently preparing two book-length studies of Indian villages, and is collaborating on the preparation of a monograph dealing with factional conflict.

About the Book

The problems of life in Gopalpur are understandable. From the Western point of view, the ways in which they are solved seem strange. How do wrestling matches between young men from different villages in the Gopalpur area help make social and economic relations between these villages smoother? Why is the preferred marital partner one's sister's daughter or cross cousin? What useful purpose can the saltmakers' caste serve when saltmakers make no salt? How are the strong forces making for competition and conflict in Gopalpur contained and controlled, so that crucial areas of cooperation are not destroyed? Why should people who live in a "simple," relatively unchanging village, see life as a "blooming, buzzing confusion"? These are some of the many questions answered in this case study that make it fascinating reading. The passing tourist sees only what to him is poverty, but life inside Gopalpur is rich. It is rich because it is complex. There are many individual choices to be made on the basis of subtle distinctions within the framework of what seems, from the outside, a simple life. Alan Beals gives us this inside view. Life in Gopalpur becomes real as the case study unfolds. And having given us this inside view, he makes it possible for us to understand that Gopalpur is one of many villages in a region of southern India where each community is like every other, yet like no other, and gives us an understanding of the forces for and against change.

GEORGE AND LOUISE SPINDLER
General Editors

Stanford, California
1962

Preface

INDIA contains not less than five hundred thousand villages. In these villages live approximately seven out of ten citizens of India, perhaps one out of every six or seven human beings in the world. The people who live in villages in India are inventive and conservative, tall and short, friendly and quarrelsome, handsome and ugly, wise and foolish, radical and reactionary. There are no typical rural Indians; there are no typical Indian villages. There are only human beings living in some relationship to the complex pattern of forces and ideas which constitute the civilization of India. To understand a single village and the people in it is to reach the beginning of an understanding of India—but it can be no more than a beginning.

The following pages describe certain aspects of the life of Gopalpur, a small village located in South India. The description is based upon a preliminary analysis of observations made by my wife and myself during fourteen months in 1959 and 1960, when we resided in the village. Our purpose in living in Gopalpur was to attempt to isolate and describe the factors which lead to the development of similarities and differences among neighboring villages. Our study was supported by the National Science Foundation. While in Gopalpur, we received assistance from hundreds of residents of Gopalpur and its neighboring villages and towns. We owe a particular debt of gratitude to Dr. K. Gnanambal of the Government of India, Department of Anthropology, who carried out a study of the neighboring village of Gannapur.

In writing this book, a certain emphasis has been placed upon the problems and insecurities faced by the people of Gopalpur. This emphasis should not be permitted to obscure the fact that Gopalpur is like any other human community. It is a place where things usually run smoothly, but where sometimes there is conflict. Men in Gopalpur sleep quietly in the shade, play joyously in the cool of evening, and sing thunderously to themselves as they follow their plows through the heavy soil. In most ways, they are like all other men; in a few ways, they are different.

A. B.

Stanford, California
1962

Contents

Tatalgiri. Its hilly location permits a photograph from above.
The houses are typical of the region and similar to Gopalpur.

Procession. Two Farmers carry pots of water decorated with leaves, while two Leather-
workers from a neighboring village beat a complex rhythm on their drums. Shanappa, the
companion of the Gauda's son, stares into the camera.

Weightlifting. There are two kinds of weights: round boulders lifted with both hands and hollow stones containing handgrips which are lifted with one hand. The arm supporting the weight must now be extended vertically upward.

Winnowing. When the wind blows, the man sitting covers his head with a burlap sack and sweeps up the grain as the standing men pour grain and chaff from their baskets.

The Shape of Gopalpur

Hanumantha

HANUMANTHA STANDS UPRIGHT in the center of a clearing. At his feet is a round granite stone considerably larger than a basketball. Over his head the leaves of a *nim* tree shift and turn in the sunlight. Hanumantha has removed his shirt and wrapped his *dhoti* around his waist, tucking it tightly between his legs so that the five yards of flowing white cloth resemble a tightly fitting pair of shorts. Deliberately, Hanumantha squats beside the stone. Seizing it with his hands he raises it up to his knee. Straightening his legs, he carries it up to his waist and rolls it up to his shoulder. Suddenly he loses control. The stone splashes into the sand as the barefooted youth dodges to one side.

In a few minutes, Hanumantha gives the stone to Sabe and sits beside me on the stone platform under the nim tree. "Is it true," he asks, "that in America people eat children?" He continues without permitting an answer, "I have heard about your country, people there don't do any work, everything is done by machines. You people are not very strong. That is why you must depend on us for food. We must work hard every day under the hot sun and even in the rain. You people work whenever you feel like working, and you eat rice every day. My brother has been to Bombay and has told me all about the way you Americans live."

"Actually," I tell him, "my country is not Bombay, it is many miles from Bombay."

"Yes," he says, "I know, it is in London."

Although he is only twenty-six, scarcely old enough to marry, Hanumantha has seen much of the world surrounding Gopalpur. He has been several times to the market at Kandkur, four miles away, and he has attended fairs and festivals in villages up to ten or eleven miles distant. He has never been to the town of Yadgiri, fifteen miles away, and is a little afraid of what might happen to him if he goes there.

Hanumantha's business is the business of almost every other adult male in Gopalpur. It is to plow the fields, to dig the gardens, and to harvest the ripened crops. The most important thing in Hanumantha's life is to find his place in the village. He must find a wife; he must have male children; he must have many friends; he must accumulate enough wealth to be able to arrange proper marriages for his children; and he must have a number of mourners at his funeral. To achieve these things, "to make his name great," Hanumantha must operate within the set of rules appropriate to success within the village. Many of these rules are unwritten and are not discussed by Hanumantha's relatives and neighbors. When someone breaks such rules, there may be little more than an increasing awareness that someone in the village is out of his proper place. When this happens, Hanumantha's neighbors take action to restore the pattern that has been warped or broken.

At the moment, Hanumantha is following the course of action suitable to a young man. By developing his physical skills as a weight lifter and wrestler, he hopes to win a coconut at a local fair and offer it triumphantly to the village god. Later, Hanumantha will learn, as the older men in the village have learned, that deeds of strength and heroism bring only a passing reward, and he will then turn his attention to the making of alliances and coalitions designed to shield his growing family from the whims of Nature and the uncontrolled impulses of his fellow men. As he moves into middle age, Hanumantha will find that the basis of success in Gopalpur lies not in physical prowess, but in the number of cattle and the number of men that he can control.

Hanumantha considers himself to be a free agent. He decides what he is going to do and he does it. At the same time, Hanumantha's freedom is limited by the context within which he operates. That context includes the natural and material environment of the village of Gopalpur; it includes Hanumantha's childhood experiences; it includes the people who live in Gopalpur and the region surrounding Gopalpur; and it includes the rules and the ways of life which have developed in Gopalpur over many generations.

The Material Environment

Using tools and techniques available to them, the people of Gopalpur have interacted with their physical surroundings to produce a material environment that is a result of their way of life and at the same time a cause of it. The buildings and walls of Gopalpur, most of which were standing when Hanumantha was born and will be standing when he dies, channel the flow of traffic through the village, and so influence the frequency with which Hanumantha will encounter particular friends or neighbors. Many other things—the distance to the nearest neighboring village, the extent to which Hanumantha's ancestors have maintained the fertility of the village fields, the kinds of things that will grow in the fields, the forces controlling wind and rain—set subtle limits upon the possible ways in which Hanumantha can behave.

Gopalpur is a mile from the nearest neighboring village. Unless he wishes to expend considerable effort, Hanumantha must find his friends and enemies within his own village. The buildings in Gopalpur are rectangular structures of stone and mud. A typical house is perhaps thirty feet wide and forty feet deep. At the front of the house, there is a raised veranda six to eight feet wide. In the center of the veranda is a large double door, set in a carved wooden frame with carved horses' heads projecting just above and on both sides of the door. There are no windows in the walls; light and air are admitted in limited quantities through holes cut in the flat clay roof. When it rains, these skylights are covered with plates and the householders sit inside in the darkness wondering when the water will find cracks in the roof and pour down into the interior.

Just inside the doorway, at ground level, stand cattle solemnly munching hay that has been removed from a platform above their heads and deposited at their feet. Further back, in the darkness of the interior, is a raised area. Here, the floor has been carefully smeared with a plaster of hard red mud brought from a nearby hillock. Into the floor has been set a mortar and millstones used for pounding or grinding grain so that it can be made into one of several varieties of mush, or into flat round pieces of unleavened bread. Behind a door leading off the platform is a kitchen. At the left of the kitchen door on the opposite side of the room, a flat stone is placed at floor level and surrounded by a rim of mud and stone. A small opening leads from the stone through the wall. Brass and clay jars full of water standing beside the stone indicate that it is a bathing place. On the other side of the room is a low platform, with two small fire places cut into it at one end. Round-bottomed pots, full of cooked food or of stored grain, line the remainder of the platform. Each pot is placed on a ring of rice straw so that it cannot tip. Smoke from the fireplace fills the kitchen and drifts into the main part of the house. Behind another door is a smaller room used for grain storage.

The house in Gopalpur is a fortress, used for cooking, the storage of valuables, and the keeping of cattle. The real business of living takes place outside, on the veranda or on the stone platform under the nim tree. People carry food outside to eat. Housewives have a second flour mill on the veranda, where they may grind grain and gossip with the neighbors. The old man spends his days sitting under the nim tree, meticulously twisting rope on his naked thigh. The baby lies on the platform, or in a cradle suspended on ropes from the ceiling of the veranda. Older children play in the dirt in front of the house, pretending to cook or plow, or enact parts in a drama or ceremony. At nightfall, the family's two cots are placed in the street or in a cleared space in front of the house. The wife sleeps in one cot with her mother-in-law and the baby. The husband sleeps in the other cot with his male children. The old man shuffles off to the fields where he sleeps on a platform overlooking the ripening crops.

In addition to the houses and stone platforms, the only structures of any importance within the village are small stone houses or shelters within which are placed the images of the various gods. The most important of these "god-houses" are those of the two village gods. One of these, dedicated to Hanumantha and his reincarnation, Bhima, is located at the southeastern edge of the village. It is surrounded by a cleared space and a low barrier. To this place come wedding parties from other villages and, on feast days, processions of people to make offerings. The other important godhouse, located outside the village, is the tomb of Shah Hussein. For generations, this god or saint has defended the village against hard times and misfortunes. Every year, when they feel happy, the young men of Gopalpur walk in procession, with drums beating, to the sacred Bhima River ten miles away. A Brahmin priest is paid ten rupees (ten days wages) to carry a potful of water from the river to wash the tomb of Shah Hussein. Scattered throughout the village are smaller godhouses. There is a termite nest dedicated to Nagappa, the snake god, and there are temples to the often present meat-eating goddesses of cholera, of small pox, and of scabies.

The Countryside

Outside the narrow compass of the village is a fence of thorns designed to protect the fields from roaming cattle. Here stand great stacks of hay used to feed the cattle during the hot dry months between March and June. Narrow passageways lead from the village down thorn-lined pathways into the fields. To the east runs a small stream, swollen with flood waters during the rainy summer season but reduced to a few stagnant pools in the hot season. At dawn and at twilight, the women of Gopalpur come to scoop out shallow pools in the sand and fill their brass water jars with the slowly gathering water. At other times, wrinkled old women wash their pet goats or water buffaloes, and small children wade in the lukewarm water and tumble in the sand. Men wrap their headcloths around their waists, wash their bodies and then their dhoties (waist cloths) and shirts. Women wrap themselves in their husbands' worn dhoties and spread their saris (eight yards of colored cotton cloth) across the sand to dry.

Beyond the stream, looking toward the market town of Kandkur, lies the finest land in Gopalpur. During the fall and early winter, these fields bear great stalks of sorghum millet, eight to fourteen feet high. At the tip of each stalk is a heavy fistful of the grain that forms the basis for almost every meal. When the watchmen are not looking, passers-by stop to cut the ripening canes and then move on, chewing the sweet pith and spitting it out along the pathway. To own one of these fields is to be rich, for every acre yields three or four crops every two years.

North of the village, the land is higher and more sandy. Scattered through the fields are great mango trees whose acid, green fruit is the only fresh food available during the hot season. In a few places, ambitious farmers have scratched shallow wells and used them to irrigate patches of onions and chili and eggplant. Closer to the village, wealthier men have built huge stone-lined wells resembling swimming pools. Older men enter these wells treading softly on slabs of granite thrust into the sides of the well to form a staircase. Younger men and children, when it is time for their weekly bath or when the weather justifies such sport, approach the well at a gallop and jump from the parapet into the water twenty feet below. The beginning swimmer's older brother attaches water wings of pithy wood to his shoulders and tosses him casually into the water.

South of the village the soil is quite sandy. In low-lying places, moisture has gathered and the land is barren and salty. Where water trickles through the salty soil, saltmakers come, collect the saltwater and pour it onto great flat stones rimmed with clay. The water evaporates, leaving behind it large crystals of off-white salt. Beyond this desert area, children six to twelve years old guide their sheep and cattle from shrub to forlorn shrub, or sit in a tree's scant shade and play forlorn melodies on their shepherd's pipes.

Beyond this pasture land, the terrain slopes gently upward toward the knife-edge of granite that marks the boundary of the village. Within the granite walls of this hill is said to be a secret cave where bandits once gathered to divide their loot. It is said that, even now a tiger lurks there. Young men sometimes come and search within the walls of the hill for bandits or tigers. In 1960, in a neighboring village, three young men found a *cheeta* (a leopard), attacked it with sickles and wood knives and, although they were seriously injured, gained a certain notoriety. Those who travel to the hill at dusk or dawn will surprise a herd of antelope and see them bound effortlessly away across stream beds and thickets.

From the top of the hill, the surrounding countryside is visible. To the north and east stretches a low range of rolling forested hills a thousand feet high. To the south and west, the plain stretches down to the gorge of the Bhima River. Fifteen miles west, hidden by hills, is the town of Yadgiri where there is a railway station and where the great officials of government have their offices. Fifteen miles east is the town of Narayanpet where people go to sell their surplus grain and to buy clothing for special occasions.

A view from the top of the hill suggests some of the limits and possibilities which result from the location of the village. Because Gopalpur is located in the center of the plain, it lacks extensive forests or grazing lands. Wild boars do not come out of the mountains to attack the growing crops, and cheetas rarely prey upon the calves or sheep. Because the streams are wider toward the center of the plain, the road from Yadgiri to the distant city of Hyderabad bypasses Gopalpur and skirts the hill slopes where stream channels are narrower and more easily bridged. Because Gopalpur has a mixture of kinds of land, the village raises three separate major crops at different times of the year. This means that people in Gopalpur must work harder and more continuously than people in nearby hill villages, where rocky soil and good drainage make possible only one thin crop per year. Because the only road to Gopalpur is a three-mile-long cart track following the sand and mud of a creek bed, government officials and outsiders rarely visit.

In addition to that portion of the physical environment which can be viewed from a hill top, Gopalpur is deeply influenced by larger forces of geography and climate. Because the plain, or rather plateau, upon which Gopalpur is located is cut up by the deep gorges of such rivers as the Bhima and separated from other portions of the great central plateau of India by forested hills and mountain ranges, Gopalpur and the region around it has always been isolated from the main streams of history. Small kings and bandit chieftains have built great fortresses on the rocky monoliths of the plains and from them have raided each other's palaces and the surrounding villages. Even now, each village is a fortress and, hidden beneath grain sacks or in dark corners of his house, almost every man has a sword, a spear, and sometimes a breast plate and shield. When people in Gopalpur were told about another village where forest officials and other minor government servants took bribes and extorted money from the farmers, the response was immediate: "If anyone tried that here, we would kill him." Recently, thirty young men from a village near Gopalpur were arrested for making an armed attack on another village some fifty miles away.

The most important deities in the Gopalpur region are Hanumantha and Bhima, different manifestations of the same violent, untamed god. Hanumantha is the monkeylike god who helped Rama, the hero of the *Ramayana*, to rescue his wife, Sita. It is recorded that Hanumantha entered the capital city of Ceylon and set fire to it by tying a torch to his tail. Bhima was the largest and most warlike of the five Pandava brothers, the heroes of another epic, the *Mahabharata*. Surrounded by a rugged and forbidding countryside and with such gods as models, the people of the Gopalpur region have maintained a way of life relatively unaffected by the distant cities.

Whether he is choosing a place to sleep at night or a particular deity to worship, the individual in Gopalpur is influenced by the shape of his village and by the shape of the countryside around his village. Hanumantha is free, but his freedom is limited by a material environment that influences not only his everyday experiences, but the history and development of his village as well. Nowhere is the influence of environment upon man more marked than in the methods used for obtaining food and the timing of work and play.

Food Production

To deal with his environment, the farmer of Gopalpur has available to him a stock of techniques and ways of acting handed down to him from his forefathers. Tools are made in the village by the farmer himself, working with the carpenter and blacksmith. The plowshare consists of a curved, sharpened piece of wood with a flattened iron spike for a blade. A long pole runs from the top of the plowshare to a wooden yoke, which is placed on top of the necks of a pair of bullocks and held there by ropes and bars of wood tied beneath the bullocks' necks. Attached to the rear of the plowshare is a wooden handle, which the farmer grasps with one hand and tilts to the left or right in order to steer the plow. Except for the iron tip, the plow differs little from the earliest plows known to history. In addition to the plow, the farmer uses a harrow, a horizontal metal blade which is drawn through the soil, as well as an assortment of rakes, seed drills, and planks. All are of simple construction: planks and pegs made with an adze by the carpenter; metal tie bands and tips beaten out of soft iron by the blacksmith; parts tied together with rope twisted by the farmer. Carts have two solid wooden wheels attached by cotter pins to an iron rod running beneath the body of the cart.

A five-acre field must be plowed at least twice, requiring eight days of labor by one man and two bullocks. Cow manure and compost must be transported from the village to the fields before the crop is sown. This is done by two men working with short-handled hoelike shovels, two baskets, two bullocks, and a cart. The preparation of the soil may take as much as thirty days, depending upon the amount of manure available, the distance of the field from the village, and the amount of energy that can be mustered at times when the temperature in the shade exceeds 110 degrees Fahrenheit. Using a harrow to break up clods and to level the soil requires another eight days of labor by the farmer and a team of bullocks.

The field is then sown in one day, by three men using a seed drill and a pair of bullocks. Some crops, rice for example, are sown broadcast. Sowing marks the climax of one to two months of steady labor. After sowing, the farmer is free to rest, to care for one of his other fields, or to hire out as a laborer. After a month, the field must be weeded and the crop thinned. The work demanded by these two operations varies depending upon the amount of rainfall and the number of seeds that have germinated. Usually, ten to fifteen people must work for three or four days to complete the weeding, thinning, and transplanting necessary to bring order to a newly planted field. After thinning and weeding has been completed, one member of the family must remain in the field at all times, day and night, to guard against theft by men, cattle, birds, and antelope. This watch must be maintained for two and a half to three months, until the crop is harvested. Harvesting, with locally made sickles, is done by ten men working for three or four days. The grain, still on the stalk, is carried to the threshing ground which has been plastered with mud and swept clean. The grain has been spread out to dry during the morning. In the afternoon, eight to ten bullocks, cows, and water buffaloes are driven around and around a stake in the center of the center of the threshing ground, until the grain is knocked off the stalks by their hooves. Hay must then be removed with a forked stick and the remaining grain and chaff swept up by the farmer's wife who fills her husband's winnowing basket and hands it up to him as he stands on a three-legged stool, shouting angrily at the coy gods who control the wind. When a gust of wind comes, he pours the contents of his basket out and the wind carries away the chaff, leaving a pile of grain directly under the basket. This is swept up by a third worker, perhaps a teen-age son, and placed in burlap sacks. While these operations vary with the kind of crop and the amount of the harvest, as a rule they require from four to seven days of labor. Later on, if beans, peas, or other legumes have been planted between the rows of grain, they too must be harvested, threshed, and winnowed.

A single five-acre field absorbs from four to six months of intermittent labor; rice fields are smaller but require more intensive cultivation, and constant attention. Most farmers in Gopalpur own a few acres of black soil land, a fraction of an acre of rice land, and a larger patch of sandy land. Each of these kinds of fields is planted at a different time of year to a different kind of crop. The farmer begins his agricultural year with *Ugadi*, the New Year festival, in March or April. During May and the early part of June, the hottest months of the year, he transports manure to those fields which are to be planted in June. Toward the end of June, the hot season ends and the monsoon rains begin. In July, the farmer plants millet and legume crops on his sandy fields. Sometimes, he lets his black soil fields lie fallow; sometimes, if he has plenty of manure, he plants a first crop on them. In August or September, if the rains have been good and the irrigation tank (reservoir) is filled with water, the farmer plants his patch of rice land. In September or October, the black soil fields are planted to "white sorghum," the major food crop of the village.

In addition to the basic millet and legume crops, there is a host of minor crops. Everyone tries to have a few mango and tamarind trees; everyone has a small vegetable garden devoted to chili, eggplant, onion, and leafy vegetables. For cash, people plant peanuts, tobacco, or cotton, or they may sell surpluses of any of the other crops. Virtually every family tries to have a female water buffalo for milk, two plow bullocks, and a few sheep, goats, and chickens for feasts and sacrifices. Except during the hot season from the end of February to the end of June, there is always more work than it is possible to do. A little more manure can be collected and added to the compost pit; a few more green branches can be cut for the goat; more time can be spent plowing and leveling the fields. If a man is really ambitious, he can plant trees or dig a well and start a garden.

Times and Seasons

Men and women in Gopalpur rise with the first light of dawn. The woman stumbles into the black interior of the house and brings out cold food left over from the day before—perhaps a jar of liquified mush to be drunk hurriedly this early, perhaps a little rice. The farmer wolfs his light breakfast and hurries off to his field, carrying his plow over his shoulder and driving his cattle before him. When the sun becomes warm and the bullocks begin to tire (10:30—11:00 A.M.), the farmer returns to the village. If the day is very hot, he comes back early in order to swim and to rinse out his clothing before eating. Otherwise, he splashes water over his legs and arms and then sits on the kitchen floor, or outside on the veranda to eat.

While the farmer plows, his wife has brought several pots of water from the stream. She has swept the house and the yard in front of the house, and carried the rubbish and manure to the compost heap outside the village. She has dried grain on the roof and ground it, swinging the stone handmill with muscular arms and the weight of her body. She has started a fire in the kitchen using only a few small sticks of wood. Over the fire, she has placed an earthen-ware pot containing chili, beans, leafy vegetables, tamarind, salt to taste and water to cover. Each day, this mixture is slightly different: the vegetables change, the beans may be fresh or dried, and of several different varieties. Whatever else the mixture may contain, it must always include an abundance of chili and a reasonable quantity of salt.

While the vegetables simmer, the housewife mixes water with sorghum flour, pats the dough into thin cakes of unleavened bread and toasts them over the fire. After pouring water over her husband's arms and legs, she serves his meal, spooning the vegetables onto the bread to make a kind of open-faced sandwich. With this basic meal, people may have a little rice, some mango pick-les, or perhaps some yoghurt mixed with water. If the water buffalo is giving milk, *ghi* (clarified butter) is poured over everything that is to be eaten.

After the meal, from about twelve to three, people sit quietly in the shade and gossip. The farmer, if he is tired, sleeps. Younger men and children play games in the shade. At three in the afternoon, nine hours after dawn by the local reckoning, men return to the fields to work until dusk. Women, too, go to the fields during this part of the day to collect grass for the cattle, or to perform light chores connected with weeding or harvesting. At dusk, people return to the village to consume cold meals by the pale light given by cotton wicks placed in clay lamps. If the moon is full, people gather in the streets. Men laugh and gossip; women form groups and sing songs and dance. If there is no moon and the night is dark, people go early to bed, and by nine o'clock the village is silent.

During the rainy season and the cold season, when such activities as weeding and harvesting are at their peak, people spend the entire day in the fields. The men are joined at noon by the women who had remained home to cook. During the sowing and harvesting seasons in particular, men do not bathe or have haircuts; they live, eat, and often sleep in their fields, taking advantage of every moment of daylight. On some days, when there is not much work in the fields, the whole family will get up while it is still dark and go off noisily with their neighbors to the forest, four miles away. There, long before the forest rangers have risen from their comfortable cots, firewood is collected in great headloads, and carried back to the village. Sometimes in the forest, young people stray away from the group. It is here, that the young man whose marriage has been too long postponed, or whose wife is too young to provide appropriate companionship, meets the housewife whose husband is too old, too disagreeable, or too dark to please her.

If there is excessive dalliance in the forest, members of the group may delay their return to the village. When this happens, they are likely to be met at the road by the forest rangers. The forest rangers confiscate blankets or shirts or headcloths of the villagers, and send them on their way. Later, these items of clothing will be ransomed for a rupee (a day's wages) apiece. Anyone who is caught by the head forest ranger is required to pay five rupees for the privilege.

During the hot season, the pattern of life in Gopalpur changes. Every night, when the moon is shining, some communal activity takes place. Once it is the puberty ceremony of a young girl, to whom the women, sitting around the honored maiden sing instructive songs. The next time, a group of older men from a neighboring village, dressed in the finery of borrowed clothing, arrive to discuss marriage arrangements with the father of one of the village girls. On other occasions, there is an all-night drama rehearsal, a visit to a wrestling match in another village, or a ceremony and feast in honor of one of the village gods. In the daytime, the village is quiet. Men sleep in the shade or in a cool corner of their house, or, for that matter, in someone else's house if it is cooler or quieter. Women hurry through their chores and, by afternoon, all are sleeping.

Mastery of the Environment

Although, at times, people in Gopalpur are oppressed by the heat of the sun, by the darkness of the night, or by rain or cold, they feel themselves to be the masters of their natural environment. Anyone in Gopalpur who is ready and able to work can earn an adequate living, and enjoy the available luxuries. Almost everyone receives three meals or more per day. Every four months almost everyone receives a shirt, a dhoti, and a headcloth, or a sari and blouse. Everyone in Gopalpur has a place to sleep and cook. There is no one who cannot afford the price of a haircut. Almost everyone manages to obtain tobacco to smoke, and betel leaves and areca nut to chew. Everyone can afford to provide a coconut, or a banana, or some sandalwood for the worship of the village gods. Any young man who needs cash for his marriage can find employment for a year as a landlord's servant. Every woman wears jewels given to her at the time of her marriage. The tax collector always receives the money due him. True, almost everyone in Gopalpur is in debt, but because the money lenders are astute and knowledgeable, the size of a man's debt is itself an index of his prosperity. Only a wealthy man can borrow large sums of money.

The fact that, at any given time, most people in Gopalpur are satisfied with their manner of earning a living and control over the physical environment, does not mean that this control is perfect. There are too many weeds, and every year the farmer sees ants and caterpillers and stem borers and antelope and rats carry off a major fraction of his crop. Although most people in Gopalpur are healthy, very few mothers can boast that all of their children are living. Malaria, cholera, small pox and bubonic plague are familiar visitors to the village. These failures in the control of the environment are not really sources of anxiety, for even in these instances, people in Gopalpur believe that they have control and understanding. Disease, for example, is considered to be a punishment for sin and a normal result of the neglect of one's responsibilities toward the supernatural world. Crop failure, flood, and disease are regarded as disasters to be dealt with when they appear in accordance with traditional techniques.

Although the material environment shapes and influences almost every aspect of life, people do not regard Gopalpur's pattern as something to be changed, improved, or fought. Things, both good and bad, are as they always have been and as they always will be. For Hanumantha, the problems of life stem, not from the material world, but from the human beings who occupy it. Hanumantha knows that his crops will sometimes fail; he knows that he will suffer from headaches and fever during the hot season. He is not concerned with increasing production so much as he is concerned with protecting his fields from thieves. He is not concerned with curing illness so much as he is concerned with preventing it by preventing sinful behavior in himself and in his neighbors. People in Gopalpur are more concerned about the mastery of human relationships, than they are about the mastery of things. This derives in part, as the next chapter will indicate, from the circumstances surrounding the birth and raising of children.

2

Childhood and Its Consequences

Birth and Family

THE BIRTH CRY of the newborn child is muffled behind thick stone walls. Only the mother and a neighbor who serves as midwife are officially concerned with the coming into being of a child. In time, this three-person group will be expanded to include not only the 540 people in Gopalpur but the thousands of people in those neighboring villages included in "our country." The place which the child will occupy within "our country" is greatly influenced by his birth into a particular household.

The household is a territorial group usually occupying a house, a patch of open space in front of the house, and lands outside the village gates. Almost invariably, the people who live in a household form a kinship group. This is either a nuclear family (parents and children), or a joint family (parents, male children, wives of male children, grandchildren). Many households contain neither nuclear families nor joint families, but the residue left behind when incompatibility, infertility, or death have shattered the original unit.

Walking down the street, the census taker comes first to a large house. In front, he sees children of all ages. On the veranda, two elderly women are grinding grain and keeping a watchful eye on a two-year-old and a newborn baby. When the women are approached, they point to an old man sitting on a stone in the morning sunshine, thoughtfully smoking an old-fashioned metal pipe.

"Yes," he says, "I will list the members of my family. You can start by carrying those two old ladies off to America. One of them is my wife. She has abused and mistreated me for over forty years." After the old man has, in this way, included the women in the conversation, and after the old man and old woman have picked at each other in the affectionate manner of old married people, the census taker discovers that there are fifteen people actually living in the household. Two sons, with their wives and children, are working in a textile mill in Bombay in order to earn money for the marriage of one of the three younger brothers. Three daughters have left the household and are living with their husbands in nearby villages. The other two brothers are living in the household with their wives and children. This is a large household, the symbol of one old man's success in life. Few other men live to see a household full of children and children's children. Out of one hundred thirteen households, only six have more than nine members.

The next household visited by the census taker is a small building clinging forlornly to the side of a larger house. Instead of a thick wooden door, the house has a rickety door of woven sticks. The clay roof is in poor repair and grass is growing out of it. The census taker hesitates—perhaps this is a cattle shed. An old woman comes through the rickety door. When she sees the visitor, she falls on the ground in front of him. With surprising strength, she seizes his foot and attempts to place it on her head. "Oh, great lord," she cries, "look at my condition; look, there is a hole in my blouse. You are a great man, surely you have an old blouse you can give me." A young man of fifteen, wearing a new shirt and a red headcloth adjusted after the rakish manner of teen-agers, comes up and shouts at the old woman, "Shut up, they are not going to give you a blouse; all they do is write, write, write." The young man begins to explain that he and his mother live alone in the house. His father lives with a younger wife on the other side of the village. The old woman points at the large house standing nearby, "Once there were thirty people in that house, this entire courtyard was filled with our cattle. I had nine children, but they are all dead." It is an old story worn thin by endless repetition. The young man screams angrily at his mother; he is the head of the family. The mother looks at her son's new clothes, "Where is the money that I hid in a jar near the stove?" The census taker steals away, forgetting to ask the old woman her age or place of birth.

Out of one hundred thirteen households, four contain only one member. Fifteen contain only two members: usually a parent and a single child struggling to perform with four hands the work of eight. Most of the households in Gopalpur contain from three to eight members. Most of them consist of parents and children. Usually, these nuclear families are located beside the houses of relatives so that they enjoy many of the benefits of the larger joint family: an aunt or grandmother who can help care for the children; an uncle or grandfather who will help to watch the fields at night.

At birth, the child's place in the world is determined not only by the wealth or poverty of his family, but also by the completeness or incompleteness of his family. Where there are many people, the child lies in state, in a cradle rocked by an older sister, a grandmother, or an aunt. The mother, relieved of her household chores, is free to rest and care for the child. In the small family, the mother must continue to prepare meals for her husband; sometimes she must continue to work every afternoon in the fields. The poor man plows with a cow instead of a bullock; his wife works beside him in the field; the baby cries neglected beneath a tree. The cow's udder hangs dry and useless; the mother's breasts yield scarcely a swallow of milk. The baby is fed on rice.

Narsamma was married thirty years ago when she was ten-years old and her husband was eighteen-years old. At thirteen, five days after her first menstruation, she began sleeping with her husband. She has been pregnant nine times that she remembers. Her first child died at the age of two, after twenty rupees had been spent for medical care. The second child died one year after birth. Fourteen rupees were spent for medical care. The third child died six days after birth. The next child, a son, died nine days after birth. The fifth child lived for three years. Ten rupees were spent for medical care. The sixth child died a few days after birth, suffering from "a kind of pain." The seventh child, a boy, lived for two years and died without benefit of medical aid. The eighth child, a boy, is living. The ninth child died two years after birth. Another woman, Sabamma, says she has been pregnant eleven times. She has eight living children. She sums up her motherhood by saying, "Thank God, those pregnancies finally stopped."

In many cases, the disappointments have been so numerous that the parents postpone the naming ceremony of the child. He does not acquire a name, a social identity, until after a year or two, when it finally seems as if he might live. A young couple's first male child is fortunate. He will be elder brother to all succeeding children; someday, he may become head of a large family. His parents will spend more money on his wedding than on the wedding of his younger brothers and expend more effort selecting his bride. The youngest child in a large family is likely to be regarded as just another burden, a misfortune thrust upon the family by the gods. Female children are welcome in most families because they provide the means of participation in the process of forming ever larger kinship circles. In a few families, where custom requires that the father of the bride pay large sums of money to the bridegroom, daughters may come to be regarded as a curse. Gopalpur's gauda, the "Village Headman" and owner of nearly one sixth of the village lands, belongs to a class, the Brahmins, required by custom to give at least one thousand rupees to the bridegroom at the time of marriage. The Gauda's brother, who inherited property in a neighboring village, had five female children and was reduced to poverty. The gauda had three male children and remains the wealthiest man in Gopalpur.

The Average Child

The ordinary child belongs to a small family. Regardless of its sex, it is wanted and loved by both parents. It spends its first twelve months in a wooden or basketry cradle suspended by ropes from the ceiling of the veranda. If anything at all is worn, it is a thin cotton shirt and a patchwork cotton cap. The infant lies on its back and stares up through round black eyes at a flock of paper birds suspended by string from a piece of cardboard. When old enough to grasp an object, a small tin or plastic rattle is thrust into its hand.

When the baby cries, the mother appears and nurses it. If it continues to cry, an older sister or brother is asked to rock the cradle. The baby is rocked vigorously until it falls asleep. When the baby is ill or colicky, or cries for no apparent reason, the neighbors gather and shout at the mother, "Give it the breast, give it the breast." Babies often cry, though they are not supposed to. Even a healthy baby is likely to suffer from heat rash, insect bites, and skin irritations.

As the child grows, and violent rocking no longer stills its cries, the older sister is again called upon. She picks up the child, sets it on her hip, and runs out to play. The mother, looking up from her place by the stove, shouts, "Don't let the child fall." There is only one other recognized danger to children—the herd of cattle returning to the village at twilight. When the mother hears the herd approaching, she runs out into the street, snatches up her children, and places them in the house. Children explore their environment riding on the hip of a mother, sister, or grandmother, or perched on the shoulders of a proud father. They do not have much opportunity to crawl, and little incentive to begin to walk: someone is there to carry them. Their infantile desires for activity are often submerged in the hypnotic swinging of the cradle.

Infants are encouraged to engage in social behavior, smiling and talking, repeating the names of people who come to visit. When the child urinates, whoever is holding the child holds it to one side. When the child can understand, it is told to go outside the door into the courtyard when it urinates or has a bowel movement. The child is weaned gradually. Mothers pride themselves on the length of time they are able to nurse their children. For the first year or two, the child learns little and is subjected to few pressures, remaining a baby for the longest possible period of time.

As the child begins to walk, the mother's treatment begins to change. When the child cries in the early morning, the mother scolds and grumbles. After breast feeding, she orders it out of the house, "Go outside and play with your sister." The child clings to its mother's sari and refuses to go. The mother picks it up and puts it outside. After an hour, the child toddles back into the house and begins to cry, the mother says, "I am cooking dinner, stay outside when I am cooking dinner. If you don't stay outside, I won't cook any dinner." When the child cries again, the mother picks it up, breast feeds it and takes it outside again. When it cries again, she says, "Will your life come to an end if I don't pick you up?" When the mother goes to get water, the child again begins to cry. The mother leaves the child alone in the house and reappears in a half hour carrying water. She serves food. The child sees everyone sitting to eat and comes over laughing. The mother picks it up to nurse. She takes a small piece of bread, mashes it in her fingers and gives it to the child, who at first refuses the bread, then takes it and throws it on the ground. The mother scolds, "You have become too proud; what have you done?"

The Play Group

Out in the street, the child joins a group of children ranging in age from two to eight years. Here, relationships are established which will be important even after death. The street, where the child lives, is a barren stretch of flat, sandy dirt, opening out here and there to form larger areas where children may play. The play area is surrounded by stone walls. Great slabs of stone left over from some forgotten housebuilding lie along the sides of the area. In places, these stones have been piled up or set on edge to form low platforms or benches. The play area is shaded by nim trees and overlooked by the verandas of neighboring houses. Pieces of farm equipment, a cart or a plow, are stored near some of the houses. Scattered about on the ground, or pushed into piles following the housewife's daily sweeping of the area in front of her house, are sherds of broken pottery, sticks, and pebbles. Elevated above the dusty world of the children are a mother grinding grain on her veranda, a father resting on a string cot, a grandmother winnowing grain and picking rocks out of her winnowing basket with a failing eye and an unsteady hand. Cattle stand near some of the houses alternating their perpetual cud-chewing with sudden twitches to ward off flies.

Sidda, four years old, is playing in front of his house with his cousin, Bugga, aged five. Sidda is sitting on the ground holding a stone and pounding. Bugga is piling the sand up like rice for the pounding. Bugga says, "Sidda, give me the stone, I want to pound." Sidda puts the stone on the ground, "Come and get it." Bugga says, "Don't come with me, I am going to the godhouse to play." Sidda offers, "I will give you the stone." He gives the stone to Bugga, who orders him, "Go into the house and bring some water." Sidda goes and brings water in a brass bowl. Bugga takes it and pours it on the heap of sand. He mixes the water with the sand, using both hands. Then "Sidda, take the bowl inside." Sidda takes the bowl and returns with his mouth full of peanuts. He puts his hand into his shirt pocket, finds more peanuts and puts them in his mouth. Bugga sees the peanuts and asks, "Where did you get those?" "I got them inside the house." "Where are they?" "In the winnowing basket." Bugga gets up and goes inside the house returning with a bulging shirt pocket. Both sit down near the pile of sand. Bugga says to Sidda, "Don't tell mother." "No, I won't." Sidda eats all of his peanuts and moves toward Bugga holding his hands out. Bugga wants to know. "Did you finish yours?" "I just brought a little, you brought a lot." Bugga refuses to give up any peanuts and Sidda begins to cry. Bugga pats him on the back saying, "I will give you peanuts later on." They get up and go into the house. Because they are considered to be brothers, Sidda and Bugga do not fight. When he is wronged, the older Bugga threatens to desert Sidda. When the situation is reversed, the younger Sidda breaks into tears.

In front of another house, Bhimsha, aged four, and Narsya, nearly three, are eating. Bhimsha is holding a brass bowl filled with mush. Narsya is sitting opposite his older brother. Bhimsha puts mush in his own mouth and then in his younger brother's mouth. A neighbor, aged three, is watching. Bhimsha turns to the neighbor, "Have you finished your food?" The neighbor replies, "I have just eaten." While Bhimsha talks to the neighbor, Narsya helps himself from the bowl. When the bowl is empty, the two brothers rise and Bhimsha says to the neighbor, "We are going to wash our hands and come back, you wait here."

Bhimsha takes Narsya's hand and they enter the house. Bhimsha comes outside carrying a brass vessel full of water. Bhimsha washes his hands, then tells Narsya to bend over so that the water won't splash on his shirt. Bhimsha washes Narsya's hands and face. Both brothers go inside and return without the bowl. In the meantime, the neighbor is gathering sand. Bhimsha says. "Let's go to the platform." At the platform, Narsya removes three roundish stones, marbles, from his shirt pocket. He gives one to the neighbor and one to Bhimsha. Narsya throws his marble toward a hole in the ground and misses. The neighbor also throws and misses. Bhimsha throws and misses. On the second try, Bhimsha's stone falls into the pit. Bhimsha asks Narsya and the neighbor to try again. Narsya's marble falls in the pit; the neighbor's marble misses. Bhimsha throws his marble and hits the neighbor's stone. Narsya smiles and says, "Wait, I will hit it too." He hits the neighbor's stone and laughs. The neighbor frowns, "I am going home." Bhimsha says, "No, hit my stone." The neighbor throws his marble toward Bhimsha's, then sits down beside Bhimsha's marble and hits it with his marble. Narsya watches—he won't hit his brother's marble. Later on, Narsya begins to cry. Bhimsha says, "Why are you crying?" Narsya says, "I want to urinate." Bhimsha removes Narsya's trousers, Narsya squats and urinates against a nearby wall and then goes into the house. Bhimsha says to the neighbor, "Come tomorrow, we will play." The neighbor says, "I will come; now I will go to my house and eat bread."

Bhimavva and Devamma, two four-year-old girls, are sitting on the ground pretending to pound rice with stones. Devamma has a broom with which she is sweeping up the pounded sand. Narsamma, aged three, is sitting with her one-year-old sister and watching. The sister begins to cry. Narsamma hits her, saying, "Keep quiet." The baby cries noisily and Narsamma picks her up and holds her against her shoulder. The baby tries to get down. When, finally, Narsamma puts her down, she begins to cry in earnest. Tears run down her dusty cheeks. Narsamma then picks up the baby and leaves the group. Devamma asks Bhimavva to go to the house and bring back her little brother. Bhimavva goes off, but returns alone. The little brother is sleeping. Devamma and Bhimavva begin to winnow sand. Devamma's baby sister begins to cry. She wants to sit on Devamma's lap. Devamma picks her up. Bhimavva asks Devamma to help her pound sand. Devamma says, "Wait, I will take my sister home and come back." She returns after a few minutes with her sister who now has a cookie in her hand. Devamma puts her on the ground and begins to help Bhimavva with the pounding. The little sister begins to cry. Devamma picks her up and the two lie down together on a rock. The baby continues to cry.

Devamma picks her up and leaves. Bhimavva also leaves. After ten minutes, Devamma returns carrying the baby, who is asleep. Bhimavva brings a brass bowl and some bread. The baby is placed on the rock and the two older girls begin to eat.

Mashamma, three years old, and Mallamma, six years old, are sitting near a cart in front of the house. There is an earthenware pot full of water, and a small tin lid containing sand on a nearby stone. Mashamma mixes sand with water. She puts the mixture in the pot. Mashamma says to Mallamma, "Go get a frying pan and come back, I shall make bread." Mallamma gets up and brings a small tin lid. Mashamma takes two stones and makes a cooking stove. She says to Mallamma, "Go and bring firewood and come back." Mallamma goes near the house and collects firewood which she gives to Mashamma. Mashamma puts the firewood into the fire place and pretends to light the wood using an empty match box.

Mallamma says, "I will give you bread dough and you can fry it." Mashamma answers, "No, I will make the bread dough; you go get some water in a pitcher." Mallamma goes inside and brings a pitcher of water. Mashamma mixes mud in the pitcher and pounds it into flat round cakes. She puts the mud on the frying pan as it rests on top of the stove. She adds firewood to the stove with her left hand and uses her right hand to mix additional mud and water.

Learning in the Group

In the play areas, children train each other. Older sisters look after baby brothers and baby sisters; older brothers care for younger brothers. The child, defeated in its attempts to play with other children, may approach an adult who is not too busy. The two-year-old who has its hair pulled by another two-year-old may retreat to the warm comfort of its father's lap. During busy seasons, the relationship between parents and children dwindles almost to nothing. The father eats and leaves the house; the mother puts food down for her children and rushes off to collect firewood, get water, or work in the fields. When the child's mother is away, a jealous older sister or one of the mother's sisters-in-law may refuse to give the child water or food, and the child will stand outside the house weeping angry tears.

Within the play group, signs of direct physical aggression are rare. Boys almost never fight among themselves and resort to violence only when harassed by an active two- or three-year-old. Girls attack boys, and indulge in malicious teasing among themselves. Some girls, Devamma for example, seem to enjoy caring for infants; others bitterly resent the infants hung like millstones around their necks. Because the noise made by a crying infant or child tends to bring adult intervention, children come to use withdrawal, threats of withdrawal, and noisy crying as a means of controlling other children. By the time a child of either sex has reached the age of four, direct physical aggression—fighting, pinching, biting—has almost ceased. Parents rarely use physical aggression against their children, although the incessant whining or persistent naughtiness of a two- or three-year-old child sometimes triggers a flash of temper and a blow. An older girl who places in jeopardy the infant under her care will be struck in parental anger.

Children have little play equipment. There are no complex mechanical toys nor books that can be used in solitude. Play with sticks and sand, stones and potsherds, usually requires the cooperation of other children. The child in Gopalpur finds that the most satisfying kind of play is social play, that the most satisfying playthings available are small animals and other small children. Everything conspires to turn the child away from manipulation of its physical environment toward manipulation of its social environment. In this latter, the child most frequently creates a family. Its play is the work of the mother and father. Every year, tons of sand are solemnly ground and made into cakes. Chickens are hotly pursued by youngsters intent upon converting them into sheep or cows. Younger boys are tied together like bullocks and permitted to pull imaginary carts and plows. Girls play mother, not with dolls, but with real babies.

Much of the currency of interaction in the play group consists of things that may be eaten. The exchange of food among children, as among adults, takes place continually. Older boys collect semiedible green fruits and inflict them upon each other and anyone else in the vicinity. Younger children make forays into their houses to obtain bread or peanuts, which they then distribute. The pattern of eating is set by the frequent nursing of infants. Older children move about the village with shirt pockets stuffed with green grain, peanuts, or bits of bread. When the pocket is empty, they enter their houses and announce, "Mother, I am hungry."

The Return to the Family

This is the moment of entrapment, the only time during the day when the mother is able to exercise control over her child. This is a time for bargaining, for threatening. The mother scowls at her child, "You must have worked hard to be so hungry." The mother serves food and says, "Eat this. After you have eaten it, you must sit here and rock your little sister." The child eats and says, "I am going outside to play, I will not rock my sister." The mother says, "You eat so much; where do you go; why won't you stay home?" The child replies, "I have a stomachache, I cannot rock my little sister." The child finishes its food and runs out of the house. Later, the child's aunt sees it and asks it to run to the store and buy some cooking oil. When it returns, the aunt says, "If you continue to obey me like this, I will give you something good to eat." When the mother catches the child again, she asks, "Where have you been?" Learning what occurred, she says, "If you brought cooking oil, that is fine; now come play with your sister." The child says, "First give me something to eat, and I will play with my sister." The mother scolds, "You will die of eating, sometimes you are willing to work, sometimes you are not willing to work; may you eat dirt." She gives it food and the child plays with its sister.

Hanumavva is a girl of five years, living alone with her widowed mother. It is dark; mother and child are lying on their cot preparing to sleep. Hanumavva says, "Mother, tomorrow let us make gruel and drink it. Let us make it together tomorrow." The mother replies, "As you say, tomorrow we will cook gruel." In the morning, the mother wakes up first and says to Hanumavva, "Wake up and sweep the house. I will pound grain and heat the mush pot and make gruel." When the housework is completed, the mother says, "I am going out to walk around the village. You stay in the house." Hanumavva replies, "I will stay here. Come back quickly; if you are slow in coming I will come where you are." As the mother walks down the street, Hanumavva joins her, "Why did you come? I told you not to come." Hanumavva says, "You came, should I be left alone?" An hour later, they return to the house. The door has been left open and a dog has eaten the gruel. The mother says, "I told you not to come after me. Now a dog has eaten all of the gruel. You are an evil one, a donkey, a liar. Because you came after me, a dog has drunk all of the gruel. How are you going to live?" Hanumavva says, "How will I live? I won't eat."

Food and Love

Almost always the child receives its food, but very often the food is accompanied by a threat. The food comes from working. He who does not work may end up eating dirt. The food is a bribe, and the mother constantly claims the privilege of withholding food. Often food is slow to come. It must be paid for by running to the store to get cooking oil or betel leaves and areca nuts. Sometimes food is obtained through incessant demands. Services provided by adults for children are always conditional.

Consider the day of the fair. Timma has been told the night before that the family is going to the fair. In the morning he runs into the street and tells everyone that he is going to the fair. When he goes back into his house, his grandmother calls to him, "Timma, we are going to the fair, but you are not going with us." Timma begins to cry. The grandmother says, "You are not old enough to go to the fair. There will be many strangers there. One of them may carry you off." Timma says, "I will stay close to you the whole time." After prolonged negotiations, during which Timma begs, cajoles, threatens, promises, and weeps, he is allowed to go to the fair. There he is given celluloid dark glasses which he wears even while sleeping. Food trips to the fair, the things that make life worth living, are to be obtained through hard work and obedience, or by begging and demanding.

Long before it has begun to walk, the child in Gopalpur has begun to develop a concern about relationships with others. The period of infantile dependency is extended. The child is not encouraged to develop muscular skills, but is carried from place to place on the hip of mother or sister. The child is rarely alone. It is constantly exposed to other people, and learning to talk, to communicate with others, is given priority over anything else that might be learned. When the child does learn to walk, adults begin to treat it differently. Shooed out of the house, its training is largely taken over by the play group. In the streets, there are few toys, few things to be manipulated. The play of the child must be social play and the manipulation of others must be accomplished through language and through such nonphysical techniques as crying and withdrawal. In the play group, the child creates a family and the family engages in the production of imaginary food or in the exchange of real food carried in bulging shirt pockets.

The child's relationships with his parents center around food and mealtime. Food is obtained by bargaining and as a reward for obedience and work. Instead of physical punishment for misdeeds, there is the threat of "no work, no food," and the fear of having to eat dirt. Love and affection are directly equated with food. To be able to give food to others is to be able to dispense love and affection. Parents behave inconsistently saying "I won't feed you," then doing so anyway. They make promises, deny that they have made promises, and then keep their promises.

The major problem of the child is the major problem of the adult, that of exerting control over the unreliable world of other people: people who die suddenly in the night, people who break their promises, people who refuse to provide food, people who refuse to attend one's wedding, people who go out at night and cut other people's crops, people who lay out their property lines through the middle of other people's fields, people who are said to come at night and kidnap others for human sacrifice.

People depend upon others and search for ways of influencing and controlling them. The child may influence others by begging, by crying, or by working. Even a young man like Hanumantha finds that hard work and physical prowess are the principal avenues for achievement. The child, the person who is not married, even the person who has brothers who are not married, has few ways of exerting control over others. The unmarried man remains a dependent part of the circle of relatives and friends belonging to his father and older brothers. The woman remains a dependent until she has children and begins to use them as a means of influencing her husband. Until a man or woman acquires his belated promotion into the world of full adults, his position within the family depends entirely upon the quality of the work that he does. The person who is weak or lazy or ill is given food, but he eats without honor and dies without care or affection. The young person seeking a place in the world, craving affection, love, and food, strives for these through hard work. For that and consequently rising family fortunes are the necessary precondition for marriage. Often, the young man must earn money for his own wedding and for his brothers, as well; the young girl must build a reputation for industry and modesty that will make her an acceptable marriage partner. After marriage, a young man becomes a person who gives food to others instead of taking food from them. If he has much to give, he will be in a position to enter the political life of the village, and he can build around his household a protective fence of powerful neighbors and relatives who will shield him from the uncertainties of human relationships. With marriage, a young man becomes an adult and he acquires a circle of relatives who, if treated properly, will help him to achieve a place of importance within the village and within the region.

During childhood, the individual acquires experience with the material and social environments surrounding him. The patterns followed by the adult in dealing with the child are the major mechanisms for transmitting the culture of Gopalpur from one generation to the next. Both the material environment and the patterns of child care can be regarded as aspects of the culture of the village. In Gopalpur, the character of childhood experience draws a connection between survival and the affectionate support of the group. The individual is brought to feel that the major securities and satisfactions of life are to be found in the acquisition of a large number of friends and supporters, and in the control of them through the use of food. The most important supporters of the individual are the members of his family. In Gopalpur, kinship, particularly kinship through marriage, is used to involve the individual in a web of relationships and to relate the village itself to other villages. This is what the next chapter is about.

opposite his older brother. Bhimsha puts mush in his own mouth and then in his younger brother's mouth. A neighbor, aged three, is watching. Bhimsha turns to the neighbor, "Have you finished your food?" The neighbor replies, "I have just eaten." While Bhimsha talks to the neighbor, Narsya helps himself from the bowl. When the bowl is empty, the two brothers rise and Bhimsha says to the neighbor, "We are going to wash our hands and come back, you wait here."

Bhimsha takes Narsya's hand and they enter the house. Bhimsha comes outside carrying a brass vessel full of water. Bhimsha washes his hands, then tells Narsya to bend over so that the water won't splash on his shirt. Bhimsha washes Narsya's hands and face. Both brothers go inside and return without the bowl. In the meantime, the neighbor is gathering sand. Bhimsha says. "Let's go to the platform." At the platform, Narsya removes three roundish stones, marbles, from his shirt pocket. He gives one to the neighbor and one to Bhimsha. Narsya throws his marble toward a hole in the ground and misses. The neighbor also throws and misses. Bhimsha throws and misses. On the second try, Bhimsha's stone falls into the pit. Bhimsha asks Narsya and the neighbor to try again. Narsya's marble falls in the pit; the neighbor's marble misses. Bhimsha throws his marble and hits the neighbor's stone. Narsya smiles and says, "Wait, I will hit it too." He hits the neighbor's stone and laughs. The neighbor frowns, "I am going home." Bhimsha says, "No, hit my stone." The neighbor throws his marble toward Bhimsha's, then sits down beside Bhimsha's marble and hits it with his marble. Narsya watches—he won't hit his brother's marble. Later on, Narsya begins to cry. Bhimsha says, "Why are you crying?" Narsya says, "I want to urinate." Bhimsha removes Narsya's trousers, Narsya squats and urinates against a nearby wall and then goes into the house. Bhimsha says to the neighbor, "Come tomorrow, we will play." The neighbor says, "I will come; now I will go to my house and eat bread."

Bhimavva and Devamma, two four-year-old girls, are sitting on the ground pretending to pound rice with stones. Devamma has a broom with which she is sweeping up the pounded sand. Narsamma, aged three, is sitting with her one-year-old sister and watching. The sister begins to cry. Narsamma hits her, saying, "Keep quiet." The baby cries noisily and Narsamma picks her up and holds her against her shoulder. The baby tries to get down. When, finally, Narsamma puts her down, she begins to cry in earnest. Tears run down her dusty cheeks. Narsamma then picks up the baby and leaves the group. Devamma asks Bhimavva to go to the house and bring back her little brother. Bhimavva goes off, but returns alone. The little brother is sleeping. Devamma and Bhimavva begin to winnow sand. Devamma's baby sister begins to cry. She wants to sit on Devamma's lap. Devamma picks her up. Bhimavva asks Devamma to help her pound sand. Devamma says, "Wait, I will take my sister home and come back." She returns after a few minutes with her sister who now has a cookie in her hand. Devamma puts her on the ground and begins to help Bhimavva with the pounding. The little sister begins to cry. Devamma picks her up and the two lie down together on a rock. The baby continues to cry.

Devamma picks her up and leaves. Bhimavva also leaves. After ten minutes, Devamma returns carrying the baby, who is asleep. Bhimavva brings a brass bowl and some bread. The baby is placed on the rock and the two older girls begin to eat.

Mashamma, three years old, and Mallamma, six years old, are sitting near a cart in front of the house. There is an earthenware pot full of water, and a small tin lid containing sand on a nearby stone. Mashamma mixes sand with water. She puts the mixture in the pot. Mashamma says to Mallamma, "Go get a frying pan and come back, I shall make bread." Mallamma gets up and brings a small tin lid. Mashamma takes two stones and makes a cooking stove. She says to Mallamma, "Go and bring firewood and come back." Mallamma goes near the house and collects firewood which she gives to Mashamma. Mashamma puts the firewood into the fire place and pretends to light the wood using an empty match box.

Mallamma says, "I will give you bread dough and you can fry it." Mashamma answers, "No, I will make the bread dough; you go get some water in a pitcher." Mallamma goes inside and brings a pitcher of water. Mashamma mixes mud in the pitcher and pounds it into flat round cakes. She puts the mud on the frying pan as it rests on top of the stove. She adds firewood to the stove with her left hand and uses her right hand to mix additional mud and water.

Learning in the Group

In the play areas, children train each other. Older sisters look after baby brothers and baby sisters; older brothers care for younger brothers. The child, defeated in its attempts to play with other children, may approach an adult who is not too busy. The two-year-old who has its hair pulled by another two-year-old may retreat to the warm comfort of its father's lap. During busy seasons, the relationship between parents and children dwindles almost to nothing. The father eats and leaves the house; the mother puts food down for her children and rushes off to collect firewood, get water, or work in the fields. When the child's mother is away, a jealous older sister or one of the mother's sisters-in-law may refuse to give the child water or food, and the child will stand outside the house weeping angry tears.

Within the play group, signs of direct physical aggression are rare. Boys almost never fight among themselves and resort to violence only when harassed by an active two- or three-year-old. Girls attack boys, and indulge in malicious teasing among themselves. Some girls, Devamma for example, seem to enjoy caring for infants; others bitterly resent the infants hung like millstones around their necks. Because the noise made by a crying infant or child tends to bring adult intervention, children come to use withdrawal, threats of withdrawal, and noisy crying as a means of controlling other children. By the time a child of either sex has reached the age of four, direct physical aggression—fighting,

3

The Problem of Acquiring Relatives

The Wedding of Krishna's Son

DURING THE AFTERNOON, some of the young men in the village construct a platform in front of the Gauda's house. The platform is canopied with brightly colored saris, borrowed from mothers and sisters. After dinner, about 9:00 P.M., the young men reappear with drums and a brilliant kerosene pressure lantern. They march in procession, followed by a horde of children, from house to house to announce the imminent performance of the dance drama which they have been practicing since harvest time. Completing their procession at the godhouse dedicated to Hanumantha, they return to the Gauda's house and disappear behind a curtain covering the veranda. While the curtain billows and moves about, several men carrying drums, cymbals, and violins, take their position on the platform. They begin to play and sing. As this overture proceeds through many repetitions and variations to its conclusion, groups of people arrive from neighboring villages. Families from Gopalpur bring out their cots and place them in advantageous positions in front of the platform.

The music stops, Gopalpur's Muslim Priest and a well-known Carpenter from a neighboring village appear on stage. Together they engage in a dialogue. The Muslim says to the Carpenter, "What are you called?" The Carpenter replies, "Called mush." When the slim store of puns and jokes has been expended, they begin to discuss the drama that is to be given. They explain who each of the characters is and reveal the plot. When they have finished, they return to the orchestra and the Carpenter picks up his violin. Following this, actors appear one by one, each making a grand entrance. Male actors wear great crowns of gold and have golden wings affixed to their shoulder blades. The women wear saris and are smothered under a weight of jewels. The actors include Farmers, Muslims, Stoneworkers, Saltmakers, and Carpenters; all are young men from Gopalpur. As each actor plays his role on the stage, people in the audience rise and shout, "Here is a rupee for so-and-so, from his aunt in Gannapur. Here are two rupees from your sister in Yelher."

In the first scene, Lakshmi's elderly relatives are assembled to discuss the possibility of her marriage to Krishna's son. They quarrel. Karna thinks that Lakshmi should be given to his own son, rather than to a poor boy. Lakshmi prays and a goddess promises her Krishna's son. In the next scene, Krishna and his wife appear. The wife scolds Krishna, "Why haven't you arranged a marriage for your son?" Krishna says, "I have arranged for his marriage to Lakshmi." The wife is scandalized, "You know that family is worthless."

Later, Lakshmi, hearing that she is to be married in five days and certain that her father has decided to give her to Karna's son, flees into the forest. She meets Krishna's son and urges him to marry her at once. Krishna's son refuses, "I cannot marry without my father's permission." When Krishna's son leaves, Lakshmi is kidnapped by giants. Lakshmi's father promises to give her in marriage to whoever succeeds in rescuing her. Krishna's son does battle with the giants and rescues Lakshmi, only to find that Lakshmi's father his changed his mind. Eventually the marriage takes place, rice is distributed among the audience, and the play ends with the audience throwing rice over the happily married couple in the cold white light of dawn.

The play is performed year after year. It is a story every child knows and its theme is the tension between two families at the time of marriage. The annual statement of the importance of marriage, and the importance of proper relationships between the family of the bride and the family of the groom, can be produced in the form of a drama only when proper relationships obtain among men of many different kinds within the village. In a sense, the play states the two most important themes of social life—cooperation among many different families within the village and cooperation through marriage among families in different villages. These two poles of social life are reflected in the contrast between the play area or neighborhood and the household. The neighborhood embodies the idea of a group of people, not necessarily related, growing up together and working together. The household embodies the idea of a set of people related by common descent and marriage. Although these two basic ideas of kinship and of propinquity or nearness are utilized as binding forces in almost all human societies, the use of these two principles in Gopalpur is so structured as to permit the individual to extend his ties to other individuals almost indefinitely.

The Great Family

The idea of kinship finds its greatest expression in the concept of *jati*. The term *jati*, which the Portuguese explorers of India translated as *"casta"* or "caste," cannot be directly translated into English. Essentially, it means breed, family, or tribe. Ordinarily, people in Gopalpur conceive of a jati as a category of men thought to be related, to occupy a particular position within a hierarchy of jatis, to marry among themselves, and to follow particular practices and occupations. In Gopalpur, it is believed that long ago a series of different jatis or breeds was given birth. Because all or most of these jatis were formed at the same time, the basic relationship between them is that of brothers. Just as a younger brother owes respect and obedience to his older brother, so members of a low-ranking jati owe respect and obedience to the members of a high-ranking jati.

It is the presence of kin relationships between jatis that makes marriage between their members impossible unless the two jatis are closely linked and their precise relationship to each other is known. A marriage between two persons who are descended from the same male ancestor in the male line (patrilineally) is incestuous. No marriage can take place until it has been demonstrated that bride and groom are from different lines of descent. The biological explanation of this, according to people in Gopalpur, is that the female has little influence upon biological relationships; she is the soil upon which the seed is sown. All patrilineally related individuals bear identical seed and their relationship is that of brother and sister.

Within any single jati, two distinct lines are implicit in the kinship terminology. Because of previous intermarriage, an individual's membership in one line or the other can be determined. For example, the mother and father of Ego, the individual, belong to two different lines, otherwise they could never have married in the first place. Ego bears the same seed as his father. Ego's mother and his mother's brother belong to the other line and carry different seed. Ego's mother's brother's daughter belongs to the seed line of Ego's mother and can become Ego's wife. Ego's father's brother's daughter carries the same seed as Ego and she is Ego's "sister." The most desirable marriage for Ego is with his own sister's daughter, for the sister's daughter cannot possibly contain the same seed as Ego. Ego's brother's daughter has the same seed as Ego, and she is classified as Ego's "daughter."

Members of the Family

The fact that women leave the household, and usually the village, at the time of marriage leads to the establishment of four major classes of relatives in terms of membership in either Line I or Line II, and in terms of sex. Relatives who are too old or too young to be involved in marriage arrangements, and who can be neither parents nor children of the bride and groom, are not classified by line membership but are simply called "grandfather," "grandmother," or "grandson," "grand-daughter." The male members of Line I include "father," "older brother," "younger brother," and "son." The terms used in Gopalpur to describe these relationships are given in Table I. The male members of Line I tend to remain permanently in the same village, neighbor-

TABLE I

The Kinship Terms

Line I		Line II	
"Father" *appa*	"Father's sister" *atti*	"Mother's brother" *mava, mama*	"Mother" *amma*
"Older brother" *anna*	"Older sister" *akka*		
Ego (M)	Ego (F)		
"Younger brother" *tamma*	"Younger sister" *tangi*		
"Son" *maga*	"Daughter" *magalu*	"Daughter's husband" *ale*	"Potential wife" *sosi*

Other terms:

1. "Grandfather," *tata;* "Grandmother," *ayyi;* "Grandson," *momaga;* and "Granddaughter," *momagalu,* all refer to relatives who are too young or too old to participate in Ego's marriage arrangements.
2. Big, *dodda;* and Little, *sanna* or *cikka,* distinguish relatives addressed by the same term. "Big father" is father's older brother.
3. "Real," *cas,* applies to mother, father, brother, sister, son, and daughter. "Co-uterine," *svadara,* applies to mother's brother, father's sister, and sister's children.
4. "Younger brother's wife, " *nadini;* "Older brother's wife," *nagani;* "Husband's older brother," *bhava;* "Husband's younger brother," *mayduna;* and "Husband's brother's wife," *nagani,* are used to specify relatives within the household.
5. "Younger sister's husband" or "Brother-in-law," *bhavumayda,* tends to be replaced by "Mother's brother" or "Daughter's husband" which do not imply equality.

Principles:

1. All relatives are classified by sex.
2. All relatives except the very young and the very old are classified by Line.
3. When a relationship is traced through descent lines, relatives are classified by generation and by relative age within the generation; when a relationship is traced through marital ties, relatives are classified by function, "Mother's brother" being "Bridegiver," "Mother" being "Who marries 'father' " or " 'Bridegiver's' sister."

hood, or household and are considered to contain the same seed as Ego. These terms are applied by extension to all males in the village. For example, Ego's father is "father," his father's brother is "father," a distant relative of Ego's father's age or generation may be "father," and the neighbor belonging to a completely different jati is a "father."

The women who grow up in the household and move away at the time of marriage are "father's sister," "older sister," "younger sister," and "daughter." These are all of the relatives who contain the same seed as Ego. Relatives belonging to Line II can be identified by the fact that they are the husbands and wives of relatives in Line I, or are the descendants of females in Line I.

When, at the age of thirteen or fourteen, Ego observes the appearance of a stranger of middle age wearing a yellow silk turban and carrying a staff, he greets him, "What, 'mother's brother,' why have you come?" If the stranger does not look wealthy and well dressed, Ego might well address him as "father," "older brother," or "grandfather." All of these latter terms imply a certain familiarity, even a kind of equality; Ego certainly does not want to suggest to this man in the impressive yellow silk turban that Ego considers him to be no better than his own father. The "mother's brother" is unquestionably superior to Ego's father, for it is the "mother's brother" who "gave" Ego's mother to Ego's father. The "mother's brother" is invariably treated with honor and deference when he visits the village; hence, a superior stranger is a "mother's brother." Although a "mother's brother" might conceivably be in fact a brother of Ego's mother, he may also be the man who married Ego's father's sister or Ego's older sister. In any case, the "mother's brother" is an older man, married to an older woman, and belonging to Line II. If the "mother's brother" has a daughter, that daughter may well become Ego's bride. In fact, Ego cannot marry any girl unless her father has been identified as a "mother's brother" or a "younger sister's husband." To people in Gopalpur, "mother's brother" means primarily "giver of the bride."

If the stranger is himself looking for a bride, or means to ask some favor of Ego, he may, in turn, address Ego as "mother's brother." If the stranger wishes to indicate that he considers himself to be a perfect equal to Ego, he may address him as "brother-in-law" meaning "younger sister's husband." If the stranger wishes to express his superiority to Ego, he addresses him as "sister's son" which also means "receiver of the bride" or "daughter's husband." Except for the term "younger sister's husband," which is rarely used and is considered rude or humorous, all men in Line II are divided into "Bridegivers," older men married to older women, and "Bridetakers," younger men married to younger women.

Women who are outside Ego's blood line are classified with equal simplicity. They are either "mothers" or "potential wives." The term for potential wife includes brother's wife, mother's brother's daughter, father's sister's daughter, sister's daughter, daughter-in-law, and lover. Any younger woman who is demonstrably not a member of Ego's line and who might conceivably marry Ego is a "potential wife." Because a "potential wife" is identified through her connection with Ego's sister or Ego's mother's brother or some other similar relative, the kinship system makes no distinction between consanguine and affinal relatives. A consanguine, or "blood" relationship, is the necessary precondition for the establishment of an affinal, or "marital," relationship. A sister's daughter is a consanguine relative before she becomes a wife. It is only when there is no close relative, when the consanguine tie is "forgotten," that relationships are traced through the marriage tie. For example, an older sister's husband is a "mother's brother," a "mother's brother's" sister is invariably a "mother," a "mother's" husband is a "father," a "father's sister's" daughter is a "potential wife." Even when one's own mother's brother's daughter and one's own sister's daughter are unavailable as "potential wives," there is always a classificatory "mother's brother's" daughter or "sister's" daughter waiting somewhere within the jati if only the relationship can be traced.

Marriage

Marriage is important to the young man of Gopalpur, not because it creates new kinship ties, but because it activates existing kinship ties. Before the marriage, the young man is merely "so-and-so's" son; after the marriage, he becomes first, someone's son-in-law, then, a father, and finally, a "bridegiver."

The decision concerning the choice of a bride is made by a man's parents, acting in consultation with the important men of the village. A marriage is a victory in the competition among villages, for every marriage that Gopalpur makes with another village activates more kinship ties and increases the ease with which Gopalpur can make future marriages in the other village. Marriage is not solely a concern of the jati and family of the bride and groom; it is a vital concern of members of other jatis. All future marriages depend upon the reputation of Gopalpur, and the friends that Gopalpur is able to create in other villages. For this reason, the village as a whole must sanction any marriage that takes place between Gopalpur and any other village, and the village as a whole undertakes the responsibility of ensuring that people from other villages get value received when they arrange a marriage in Gopalpur. In addition to facilitating further marriages, the existence of marriages between Gopalpur and other villages makes it possible for men from Gopalpur to validate their status in other villages. If a man goes from Gopalpur to a related village, a woman from Gopalpur is there to recognize him and establish his reputation. The existence of marital ties facilitates all economic transactions, both on a village and on an individual level.

A man's standing in Gopalpur is partly a function of the number of kinship ties which he can claim with other villages. The quality of a man's relatives is equally important, the most obvious goal of a marriage being to develop a relationship with a wealthy landlord. The individual who is able to activate a wide variety of kinship ties also has a wider choice in arranging marriages for his sons and daughters. This means that the bride or groom selected is likely to be closer to the ideal than is the case when the range of choice is smaller. At the same time, the larger the field from which the selection is to be made, the greater the danger that a rebuffed relative will pick a quarrel. For this reason, parents do not approach each other directly. The preliminary arrangements for the marriage are placed in the hands of an intermediary trusted by the parents of both parties. The intermediary is, inevitably, a successful man with many kinship ties and a position of trust and authority within the village.

The Arrangement

Boda is a tiny hamlet located about fifteen miles from Gopalpur. During the long months of 1958, the father and mother of a young man from Boda search vainly for a bride for their son. Going out together whenever they have the leisure to do so, the father and mother travel from village to village visiting relatives, seeking assistance in finding a suitable bride. In April, they come to Gopalpur accompanied by a distant relative of Sidda's wife who has offered to serve as intermediary. At Sidda's house, they say, "We have a boy, you have a daughter, are you ready to give us your daughter?" Sidda and his wife reply, "We will come see your house and property." In Boda, Sidda and his wife examine the household carefully. The bridegroom has adequate lands, a three-room house, and two bullocks. He is good-looking; that is to say, he appears strong and hard-working. On leaving Boda, Sidda says, "We are ready to give you our daughter; set a date and we will discuss the matter."

On a Monday evening, the family of the groom, accompanied by a band and drummers, arrive in Gopalpur and take their place in the Hanumantha godhouse. Sidda's family sends word around that one man from each house in Gopalpur should come to witness the arrangement of the marriage. In particular, the village officials must be present. At ten o'clock, as a crowd gathers in front of Sidda's house, someone asks if the Stoneworker jati has been invited. A young man on the dark outer fringes of the crowd announces that the Stoneworkers are present. When all have gathered, and the bridegroom's family has been brought in procession from the godhouse, one of the village officials, somewhat like a Town Crier, says "Where have you come from, why have you come?" The leader of the groom's party, an official of Boda, replies, "We have come to eat sweets." The Crier turns to Sidda, "Have you got sweets in your house; they have come to eat." Sidda answers, "If they have come to eat sweets, let them eat."

A man from Gopalpur asks, "What does a wedding cost in your village?" The people from Boda reply, "Ask instead what a wedding costs in your village; how many saris must we give you?" The Crier answers, "On our side, it is one hundred twenty-five rupees. Are you ready to give this much or not?" The groom's party replies, "Yes." The Crier continues, "We must also be given a silver anklet, a leg chain, a silver waist belt, a silver upper-arm bracelet, and gold earrings. There must be one sari worth twenty rupees and one sari worth thirty rupees. There must be thirty measures of rice mixed with dried peas." As each item is listed by weight or price, the groom's party agrees.

To signify final agreement, the groom's party offers ceremonial gifts to the bride. The bride and a "younger sister" are brought from the house and made to sit cross-legged on a blanket. A sari and two blouses are placed before the bride together with a brass plate filled with offerings of rice, dried dates, betel leaves, areca nut, brown sugar, and half a coconut. Lamps arranged with flowers on a brass plate are brought from the bride's house and placed before her. The bride is dressed in the new sari and blouse, and her "younger sister" is given one rupee and a blouse. Next comes, "the filling of the stomach": the bride's new sari is knotted to form a sack over her stomach and the opening is filled with two halves of a coconut stuffed with rice, areca nut, and dried dates. After this, saffron powder is placed on the foreheads of the two girls and on the foreheads of the bystanders. Brown sugar is then distributed among the witnesses in the order of their importance. First, some sugar is set aside for the Gauda, then for the Police Headman of the village, then for the Village Accountant, then for the Crier. Next, sugar is given to the Blacksmith, Carpenter, and Priest, who represent vegetarian jatis. After this, visitors from other villages receive sugar, and then there is a general distribution. Everyone returns to his house. After one or two hours, friends and relatives of Sidda's family return and are fed a mixture of brown sugar and rice. Again, in the morning, friends and relatives gather and eat.

Sidda's standing in Gopalpur will be affected by the number of people he is able to feed. A really great man, the Gauda, for example, is expected to feed everyone. An ordinary man must slight some of his neighbors and ignore some of his kinfolk. This is equally true of the succeeding stages of the wedding ceremony. Sidda's family will make a second trip to Boda. The family in Boda will be required to furnish hospitality to their friends and kinsmen. In a few weeks, the groom's family will come from Boda with a large entourage and again take up residence in the Hanumantha godhouse. The wedding ceremony is a larger version of the betrothal ceremony. Both the bride and groom participate and more people must be invited.

After the wedding ceremony, at which the bride and groom often see each other for the first time, the bride leaves Gopalpur with the groom's family. The bride is likely to be nine or ten years old, the groom is likely to be between fifteen and twenty-five. Until the first menstruation, the bride will probably be a frequent visitor to Gopalpur. When she menstruates for the first time, the groom's family will return her to her parents and a nine-day ceremony will be held marking the maturation of the bride. After the ceremony, the bride and groom return to the groom's village and take up normal sexual relationships. When the wife becomes pregnant, it is likely that she will return to Gopalpur to give birth to her first child. Later, as the wife forms more and more attachments in her husband's village, she will visit her parents less and less frequently.

For many people, the marriage arranged so carefully and celebrated at such cost proves unsuccessful. Men, unable to wait for the maturation of their brides, form alliances with other women. Women, bored by their aging husbands, form attachments to younger men. Sometimes, an angry husband strips his wife of her jewelry and sends her back, weeping, to her own people. A wife, searching for something which she cannot find in her husband, runs away with another man or seeks shelter with her parents. When this happens, the groom's party comes again to Gopalpur to demand the return of their bride, or at least of the jewels the bride was wearing when she escaped. Flanked by his relatives and by distinguished men from his own village, Basava, a young shepherd from a nearby village, came one day to Gopalpur. Even though she had been locked up in the house, and even though his brothers had beaten her vigorously. Basava's wife had fled to Bombay to live a gay life there until the police caught her and sent her home. Now she was living in her father's house and earning twenty rupees a week through prostitution. Seated on a stone platform, the relatives and the leading men of two villages discuss the unfortunate affair. Basava passionately desires the return of his wife. The wife's father denies that she is in the village and takes the position that Basava and his relatives must themselves find his wife. Twice, Basava and his relatives come to Gopalpur and are turned away without a wife and without a refund of the marriage expenses. The third time that Basava comes to Gopalpur the rumor is beginning to spread that people in Gopalpur do not live up to the marriage contract. Close friends of the wife's father shift their position in argument. Eventually, the marriage expenses are repaid by the wife's father, and Basava leaves Gopalpur, flaming passion having been damped out by the legalistic arguments of old men.

Divorce and death are the great countercurrents running against the requirement that all men and women should be married. The person who has been divorced or widowed is obligated to marry another person of similar status. A man must pay a high price to marry a woman who is divorced or widowed, nearly three times that of a normal marriage. Many men are forever excluded from the normal processes of social life by unfortunate marriages. For the first wife a man may have to work for a wealthy landlord for a year. For his second, he may have to work for three years, while his fields are ravaged by tenants and his house becomes dilapidated.

Implications

Marriage represents the intersection of everything that matters to the young man, to his family, and to the village itself. Just as the infant's early needs for affection and food are dependent upon a mother who alternatively feeds it and threatens to refuse food, so the young man's needs for a suitable marriage come also to depend upon a woman, usually upon a strange woman from another village. The advantages of marrying a sister's daughter or a mother's brother's daughter over whom one may exercise control are obvious, but it is not easy to find such a relative who is the right age. When a child is born, the head of the household must begin to think of ways of ensuring the happy marriage of the child. From a practical standpoint, happily married children who have lands and cattle are the only guarantee a man has that he will receive support in his old age. From a religious standpoint, attending to the needs of one's family is a sacred duty.

Within the village, a man's relatives consist mainly of patrilineally related men, his "fathers" and "brothers" belonging to the same lineage. Sometimes, there are members of other lineages, some related to him patrilineally, some belonging to Line II. Outside the village, he has his wife's relatives, his mother's relatives, his sister's relatives, and his father's sister's relatives. Any or all of these relatives, if relationships are properly maintained, can serve as a link in an expanding chain of relationships. As a man extends his chain of relationships, his power and influence increases. He is able to arrange marriages for others, even for members of other jatis, because he is known throughout the region and has important relatives in many villages. Wherever he goes, he and his companions are assurred of a warm reception. When he speaks in Gopalpur, people listen.

Such a man, a man who has "made his name great," maintains his connections with his many relatives by constantly feeding and entertaining them. His sisters and daughters visit Gopalpur frequently. They receive gifts, and their husbands are entertained when they come to call their wives back to their villages. To legitimatize and maintain a wide circle of relatives, a man must possess wealth. He acquires such wealth through the cooperation of his relatives and neighbors in Gopalpur. Here, there is a special problem, for in the process of activating relationships through marriage, he is in direct competition with members of his own and fraternally related lineages in Gopalpur, and in the process of acquiring wealth he is in direct competition with every other man in Gopalpur. Marriage ties are intrinsically valuable because they lead to such possibilities of exchange as the marriage of a daughter's daughter to a son. However, there appears to be little value in ties between two men who are "brothers" only in a distant and classificatory sense, and are, in fact, competing for wealth in the muddy fields of Gopalpur. The maintenance of fraternal and neighborly relationships within Gopalpur depends upon a delicate balance of relationships between jatis. The problem of maintaining these nonkin relationships is the subject of the next chapter.

4

Jati and Village

Kinds of Jatis

FROM TIME TO TIME, the Goldsmith and his family visit Gopalpur. They take over a small Muslim godhouse, used in other seasons as a school house, and set to work making and mending silver and gold ornaments. Compared to other persons who live a migratory life, the Goldsmith and his family appear to be wealthy. Their clothing is new, and the family seems able to purchase and consume vast quantities of meat and palm beer (the fermented sap of the toddy palm). In the course of conversations, it develops that the Goldsmith and his kind labor under a curse stemming back to a quarrel between the two deities, Visvamitra and Monesvara. Long ago, Visvamitra announced that his weight was equal to that of three hundred sixty thousand gods. Placed in charge of testing this extraordinary statement, Monesvara used scales which gave false measure.

Visvamitra, who, in fact, did outweigh three hundred sixty thousand gods, was offended and placed a curse upon all the descendants of Monesvara. These descendants, composing the jati of the Goldsmith, are required to wander continually from place to place. Whenever they earn any money, they must spend it immediately in the place where they earn it, upon such transitory goods as beer, meat, and cigarettes. It may be that this curse serves the Goldsmith as an incentive to avoid giving false measure when he weighs gold and silver. In any case, the curse and the story behind it represent the special attribute of the Goldsmith jati in Gopalpur.

Not all people in all jatis are familiar with the story of their jati. Everyone is aware that his jati has distinctive features which give it a special place in the economic, social, and ceremonial life of the village. Not all jatis that are important in Gopalpur are actually resident. The village takes its life, not just from the people who live in it, but from the many people of many different jatis who wander through the village at various times of the year, or who live in neighboring villages and come into Gopalpur to perform particular services. Sometimes, Deerhunters appear, spread nets in the fields, consume the deer or antelope caught in the nets, and disappear. Sometimes, men come who sell musical instruments. No one in Gopalpur knows their names or where they come from. All that is known is that they come every year, usually in December. Beggars, performers, tinkers, and religious mendicants—strange men and women of every description—pass through Gopalpur. Services are performed, gifts or payments are received, and the strangers pass on. They are part of the village life, but they are not of the village. No one knows who they are or where they go, but they must be sheltered and fed before they move on to the next village.

In a different class are persons who come into Gopalpur from neighboring villages to perform services. Gopalpur has no resident member of the Washerman jati. The right to cleanse clothing ritually and to provide clean cloth for ceremonies is reserved to a Washerman resident in a neighboring village. No other Washerman may serve Gopalpur. Gopalpur's Singer, the man who chants religious songs on ritual occasions, lives in a neighboring village. Singers are the special representatives of Hanumantha, the patron deity of the region. Each Singer is assigned to a particular village and has the exclusive right to collect gifts there on Saturday, the special day of Hanumantha. Despite the fact that no ceremony is complete unless the Singer is present, and despite the fact that Singers are the most important religious functionaries in the region, they are regarded as unclean and are ranked with other unclean carrion-eating jatis.

Gopalpur's Astrologer, who belongs to a high-ranking jati and is classified as a Brahmin, lives elsewhere and enjoys the exclusive right to serve as Astrologer for three villages. He predicts the success and failure of particular crops and reads the horoscopes of men and women at the time of marriage. The presence of the Astrologer is necessary for any important ceremony. Only he can fix the time of a wedding or certify that a new year has actually begun. Until recently, Gopalpur's Muslim Priest (*mavla*) lived in another village. He moved to Gopalpur in order to take up a second hereditary privilege of his jati, that of serving as Police Headman of the village. The Police Headman is a kind of executive assistant to the Gauda, who is considered to be too busy with religious and other matters to concern himself with day-to-day administration. Gopalpur's Muslim Priest serves three villages. Every year at harvest time, often in the company of Brahmin and Lingayat Priests, and Singers, the Muslim Priest goes to the threshing grounds of his villages and collects the grain due to his particular deity.

At least fifty distinct jatis are known to people in Gopalpur. Almost every one of these jatis has a definite economic, social, and ceremonial role within the village. A person desiring to establish his position within the village must know not only the characteristics of his own jati, but he must be familiar with the relationships of his jati to all other jatis. Mistakes made in dealing with members of other jatis may lead to a withdrawal of their services. A man must give grain to the Singer on Saturday, when the Singer comes to the door of his house. If he does not do so, he may have difficulty in holding any kind of ceremony essential to marriage, entertainment, or the curing of illness, and may find himself in economic trouble as well. On any other day or to any other but the village Singer, he need not give gifts.

Jati Rank

The essential distinctions that apply to all jatis have to do with the foods they eat and with the kind of occupation they traditionally follow. In theory, all things in the universe, including all human activities, are ranked in terms of what might be called nearness to God, or nearness to divine purity and order. The highest-ranking gods are vegetarian gods. Direct access to these gods is restricted to members of vegetarian castes who are sufficiently pure to handle sacred images without danger to themselves. The notion of jati purity derives from the extent to which the traditional diet and occupation of a jati conforms to the ranking of things and actions along a scale of purity–pollution. Death is polluting and body wastes are polluting, but all products of the cow are pure. Occupations that involve killing things, or touching such polluted things as hair or dirty clothing, are ranked below occupations that involve the touching of pure things.

Vegetarians are assigned a high rank because they live, in theory, without taking life. Another aspect of jati is based upon the giving and taking of food. Members of a jati can accept any food prepared by members of a higher-ranking jati, but they can accept only certain types of food from members of a lower-ranking jati. Thus, the ranking of a jati among the fifty or more jatis of the region can be established by observing which jatis are permitted to prepare and serve such foods as rice to members of other jatis. The highest-ranking jati in Gopalpur is that of its Brahmin Gauda. Ranked in order below the Brahmins are the Lingayat Priests, the Lingayat Farmers, the Carpenters, and the Blacksmiths (see Table II). Each of these jatis is represented in the village by a single family.

Lingayats represent a particular religious sect divided into a number of separate jatis. Lingayats eat together, regardless of jati, because all are vegetarians. Lingayat jatis do not intermarry. The special characteristic of the Lingayat sect is the worship of Shiva, more particularly of Basava, the bullock who serves as a conveyance of Shiva. Both the Carpenter and Blacksmith jatis are linked together in a larger jati which may be called the Artisan jati.

The next great group of jatis, representing most of the population of Gopalpur, consists of what might be called "clean" or "pure" meat eaters. The highest-ranking of these are the Saltmakers, who claim to be above Farmers and Shepherds, on the grounds that they drink only distilled liquor, not palm beer. Farmers rank slightly higher than Shepherds because Shepherds handle and cut the dead, and therefore unclean, wool of sheep. Members of the Saltmaker,

Farmer, and Shepherd jatis form the bulk of the respectable and dominant "middle class" in Gopalpur. They eat sheep, goats, chicken, and fish, but they do not touch pork or beef. The village Crier is always chosen from a particular family of Saltmakers. The "Boins," who keep order at ceremonies and handle sacred objects, are chosen from particular families of Farmers. Shepherds serve as priests for certain deities and have the task of butchering and sacrificing animals offered to Hindu deities.

TABLE II

POPULATION OF GOPALPUR

Jatis	People	Households	Lineages of males
Brahmin	4	1	1
Lingayat Priest	2	1	1
Lingayat Farmer	1	1	1
Carpenter	9	2	1
Blacksmith	3	1	1
Saltmaker	51	12	3
Farmer	227	48	5–6
Shepherd	105	23	4–5
Barber	9	2	1
Muslim Priest	7	1	1
Muslim Butcher	5	2	2
Muslim Weaver	7	2	1
Stoneworker	62	14	1
Basketweaver	10	2	1
Leatherworker	1	1	1
	503*	113	25–27

* The total population given here is a minimum figure. A census based upon householder's reports, concerning the number of people living in their house, yields a figure of 550, which includes visiting relatives, persons away on trips, and sometimes persons who have died.

Barbers and Muslims rank slightly below the three middle-class jatis, but they are generally treated as equals. For that matter, the occasions when members of one jati fail to treat members of another jati with a kind of easy familiarity are relatively rare. The existence of fine distinctions between jatis is recognized, but people in Gopalpur don't care much for fine distinctions. Muslims are divided into three jatis: Priests, Butchers, and Weavers. These jatis sometimes intermarry, but the hereditary title and occupation remains in the male line. Integration of Muslims, and, more recently, of Christians, into the system of jati relationships has always been complicated by the fact that both the Christian and Muslim criteria of pollution are different from those of other jatis. Both jatis consume beef, but not carrion beef. Among other things, Muslims do not eat pork and Christians do not drink alcoholic beverages. A further complication is that both Muslims and Christians have always possessed great political power. The region in which Gopalpur is located has been ruled for centuries by Muslims.

In fitting Muslims into the hierarchy of jatis, people in Gopalpur tend to fix their attention on the fact that Muslims do not eat pork nor the meat of animals that have died as a result of disease or old age. Jatis such as the Shepherds and Farmers, which consume pork in other parts of Southern India, do not do so in the Gopalpur region. Evidently to accommodate their Muslim rulers, people have modified their religious beliefs away from the notion that consumption of beef is polluting toward the notion that consumption of pork or of carrion is polluting. For this reason, Stoneworkers and Basketweavers, who consume pork, are ranked below Muslims in the hierarchy of jatis. Both these groups, which might be classified as "unclean meat eaters," are required to live on the outskirts of the village.

"Dirty meat eaters," the lowest-ranking of the jatis, are represented in Gopalpur by a single old lady from the Leatherworker jati. Members of this jati eat beef and pork. Their traditional duty involved removing dead animals from the village streets, eating the meat, and using the leather to make sandals and drums. The single Leatherworker presently living in Gopalpur is employed by the Gauda for the purpose of cleaning his latrine, the only latrine in Gopalpur. At one time, Leatherworkers were more numerous in Gopalpur, but they moved to a neighboring village after being converted to Christianity. Since then, people have removed their own dead animals from the streets with considerable resentment. Because converts to Christianity continue to make sandals, people of other jatis claim that they are not "real" Christians. "Real" Christians, missionaries or government officials, are regarded as persons of high status, comparable to Muslims, while converts are considered to be Leatherworkers posing as Christians. The system of jati rankings involves flexible acknowledgment of political and economic power.

Class vs. Jati

It is a mistake to assume that there is a direct correlation between the rank of a jati in terms of purity–pollution and the social and economic position of a jati or of individuals in a particular jati (see Table III). Birth into a particular jati is a reward for virtue accumulated in a previous life, but, in theory at least, one does not continue to receive the rewards after one has ceased to be virtuous. Anyone in any jati can be poor. If one is born a Brahmin, one derives certain advantages. Brahmins may always earn a little money by serving as priests; such occupations as Village Accountant are reserved for a particular class of Brahmins. A Brahmin who begs from door to door will always receive a little more than other beggars because a Brahmin is always a religious mendicant rather than an ordinary beggar. There are a relatively large number of ways in which a poor Brahmin may become wealthy.

TABLE III

POSITIONS OF THE JATIS IN TERMS OF CEREMONIAL
RANK AND ECONOMIC STATUS

Ceremonial Rank	Economic Status		
	Landlord	Middle class	Landless
Vegetarian	Brahmin	Lingayat Priest Carpenter Blacksmith	Lingayat Farmer
Mutton, no Beer		Saltmaker– – – – – –	–Saltmaker
Mutton and Beer		Farmer – – – – – – – – – Shepherd – – – – – Barber	–Farmer –Shepherd
Beef, no Pork		Muslim Priest Muslim Butcher Muslim Weaver	
Pork, no Beef		Stoneworker– – –	– – Stoneworker Basketweaver
Beef and Pork			Leather worker

Partly due to sheer numbers, there are probably as many wealthy Shepherds and Farmers in the Gopalpur area as there are wealthy Brahmins. The social class of landlords—people who own so much land that they do not have to farm it themselves—draws its membership from Brahmins, Lingayats, Shepherds, Farmers, and Muslims; but in a single village, landlords will be drawn from only one or two jatis. Wealth and social standing stem partly from jati membership, but also from political power, intelligence, and hard work. The middle class in Gopalpur consists of small farmers, who own and farm from five to twenty acres of land, and specialist or professionals who happen to have a large or profitable clientele. The middle class, in social and economic terms, includes members of every jati except the Basketweavers and Leatherworkers (see Table III). Anyone in any jati can come to own five acres of land and a pair of bullocks. Basketweavers are excluded from the middle class because basket weaving is not a profitable profession, and they find it difficult to accumulate sufficient capital to purchase land.

The lower class or laboring class in Gopalpur, composed of people who earn most of their income through agricultural or unskilled labor, is drawn from a wide range of jatis. However, laborers belonging to the Brahmin, Carpenter, and Blacksmith jatis are rarely found, because the region does not contain enough of these specialists to fill the demand. Possibly the chronic shortage of members of some specialized jatis, particularly the Brahmins, can be traced to particular social institutions. For example, the father of a Brahmin girl must pay a large sum of money, usually more than one thousand rupees, to the groom. The daughters of poor Brahmins may never marry. Even if a Brahmin girl is married, she may find herself a widow before she reaches puberty. Unlike most other jatis, Brahmins do not permit the remarriage of women who have been divorced or widowed. Another factor in the continuing shortage of vegetarian specialists is that the members of the higher-ranking or priestly vegetarian jatis are usually literate. This means that they have relatively easy access to positions in government and tend to move out of the village in search of employment. The Gauda's two adult sons have left the village permanently.

At the other end of the scale, despite the fact that most of the Stoneworkers in Gopalpur have achieved land ownership and middle class status, there is far more friction when a Stoneworker tries to improve his economic position than there is when members of higher-ranking jatis try to do so. One group of Stoneworkers purchased rice land from the Village Accountant. Afterwards, one of the young men began to plow the field. A group of Farmers and Shepherds attacked him with cudgels. According to the Stoneworkers, the young man would have been killed if an important man from a neighboring village had not passed by and stopped the beating. The Stoneworkers were compelled to buy inferior land in another part of the village. While this kind of discrimination does not appear to be the result of any particular policy, repercussions are likely to be slight when a Stoneworker is beaten. Anyone who wishes to improve his economic position must be prepared to defend his gains against jealous neighbors. Anyone who buys land is limiting his neighbor's opportunities to buy land. Most people safeguard themselves by tying themselves through indebtedness to a powerful landlord who will give support when difficulties are encountered.

Links between Jatis

Because Gopalpur contains only a fraction of the total spectrum of jatis and is dominated by jatis of approximately equal status, the economic significance of jati membership lies not so much in the restrictions that jati membership places upon an individual's capacity to improve his economic position, as in guaranteeing economic cooperation outside the family circle. For the farmer, it is good business to be on good terms with someone who owns a large flock of sheep, for this provides access to a source of manure. Basketweavers, Carpenters, and Blacksmiths are sources of farm equipment. Delay in repairing a cart or plow, or inability to obtain a basket to carry manure to the fields, can make the difference between the success or failure of agricultural operations. Typically, the farmer is rich at harvest time, poor at sowing time. He must depend upon goodwill and credit in order to survive.

For essential services, the farmer tends to enter into a contractual relationship with the specialist. The Carpenter, Blacksmith, Barber, and Potter receive fixed quantities of grain at harvest time. In return, they provide services. Most individuals in Gopalpur wash their own clothing; a few have a permanent arrangement with the Washerman. The priests of the various deities do not ordinarily receive a fixed amount. They tend to be given grain in accordance with the quality of the harvest. The priests and their gods are expected to provide a good crop; if they do not do so, they cannot expect much grain in compensation. As a good businessman should, the farmer tries to maintain a friendly relationship with all relevant deities. Even a minor deity can spoil a crop or cause illness in the family. The Singer serving Hanumantha, the Mavla serving Muslim deities, the Brahmin serving Hindu deities, the Jangama serving the Lingayat deities, and anyone else who has any kind of priestly function in connection with any kind of godhouse, can expect to receive some sort of gift at harvest time. The tax collector, the landlord, any poor person, anyone who appears at the threshing ground receives his due.

The magnificent generosity of the harvest season enables the farmer to purchase the goodwill, credit, and protection that will enable him to carry on long after his grain storage bins are empty and long after the generosity of the harvest season has been replaced by the bleak stinginess of the man who lives on credit. Most people in Gopalpur are farmers who occasionally supplement their income by taking advantage of traditional specializations and privileges. The fact that the Farmer jati maintains friendly relationships with the Carpenter jati is easily explained in economic terms. The fact that the Farmer jati maintains friendship with the Saltmaker jati is not so easily explained. Saltmakers produce very little salt. In any case, salt can be purchased at any little shop in any village or town. Saltmakers and Farmers are both farmers and there is no real necessity for an exchange of services. People say, we must be friendly with all other jatis because each of the other jatis contributes something essential to our economic well-being. This is what people say to each other, but it is not altogether true.

To fill the gap between reality and the ideal pattern of economically cooperating jatis, there are social and religious obligations. To arrange a marriage, to set up the doorway of a new house, to stage a drama, or to hold an entertainment, the householder must call upon a wide range of jatis. The entertainment of even a modest number of guests requires the presence of the Singer. The Potter must provide new pots in which to cook the food; the Boin from the Farmer jati must carry the pot; the Shepherd must sacrifice the goat; the Crier, a Saltmaker, must invite the guests. To survive, one requires the cooperation of only a few jatis; to enjoy life and do things in the proper manner requires the cooperation of many.

Even in the economic field, cooperation extends far beyond any kind of formal arrangement. Fences, constructed of dried thorny branches, soon deteriorate. When the farmer is away, there is nothing to stop the herdsman from turning his cattle into the farmer's field. When the herdsman is away, there is nothing to stop the farmer from casting stones at the sheep that strays into his field. The belief that jatis are related to each other, like brothers, and that all jatis provide essential services for each other creates a unity within the diversity of jatis.

Being Together Separately

The apartness and togetherness of jatis is illustrated by the rules governing formal meals. The basic rule is that members of different jatis should not eat together. In particular, one should not eat food prepared by members of lower-ranking jatis. Such rules imply that there can be no close association among individuals belonging to different jatis, but such terms as "food" and "eating together" do not have the same meaning in Gopalpur that they have elsewhere. "Food" refers to particular kinds of food, principally rice. "Eating together" means eating from the same dish or sitting on the same line. To people in Gopalpur, the European father who sits at the head of the table would be considered to be eating alone in stately isolation and purity. Members of quite different jatis may eat together if they eat out of separate bowls and if they are facing each other or turned slightly away from each other. Fried foods, including the millet bread which is eaten every day, can be prepared by almost anyone and eaten by almost anyone. Even these rules apply effectively only to the Brahmin Gauda and to the Leatherworkers.

Members of intermediate jatis are quite casual about the rules, so that the outsider, who observes that people in Gopalpur eat together all of the time and continually take food from each other, is likely to be confused when people assert that they take food only from members of their own jati and higher-ranking jatis, or that they never eat with members of other jatis. The rules apply to specific ceremonial occasions when the functional apartness and togetherness of the jatis is being emphasized. They do not apply to everyday life. In other parts of India, jatis sometimes have headmen or groups of elders who are charged with enforcing rules designed to maintain the ceremonial purity of the jati. In Gopalpur, there are no such agencies. Unless one has few friends and many enemies, the rules can be broken with impunity.

Every year, the families of Gopalpur gather together in the field surrounding the shrine of Shah Hussein. The only families which do not attend are the few vegetarian families in the village. Young men appear with shovels and dig trenches in the soil, with small firepits leading off the trenches at right angles. About four in the afternoon, women appear carrying rice and cooking pots. Each family takes it position around one of the firepits and each jati occupies its own trench. After ceremonies in honor of the village god and the sacrifice of chickens, goats, and sheep, each family prepares food. Everyone eats together, but separately.

The members of any one jati are relatives. They owe each other the respect, affection, and obligations specified by the nature of their kinship ties. Men of the same age in any one jati are usually "brothers." "Brothers" do not compete with each other. They do not wrestle with each other. They do not argue or debate among themselves. If the situation is even vaguely competitive, the "younger brother" always loses. If a "younger brother," no matter how distantly related, forgets himself, violence is often the result. To make matters more complicated, there are only a few men of the same age within any age group within the village. In his search for a friend or for a group of friends, the individual must either step out of the role of kinsman or out of the role of member of his particular jati. Men whose formal relationships to each other are unequal become equals when they join an informal group of friends. Men who grew up together, passing through the stages of life at the same time, enjoy a relationship in many ways more sacred and more important than the differences between jatis or between "older brother" and "younger brother." The Singer chants the story of Somarayya and Bhimarayya:

Somarayya had never been to Bhimarayya's house. Bhimarayya had never been to Somarayya's house. They had never entertained each other. They had exchanged a few words and become friends. Nobody knew they were friends. They lived quietly and happily chatting with each other every day.

One day, Somarayya's wife, on her way to purchase some betel leaves, walked past the place where Somarayya and Bhimarayya were standing. Looking at her, Bhimarayya fell in love. He said to Somarayya, "Who is that woman? If you don't know, ask someone who she is. All of my thoughts are on her. You must bring her here for a night with me. I will spend the night with her and pay her whatever she asks."

Somarayya thought, "If I say that she is my wife, then our entire relationship will be ruined. God, what a problem you have given me. If I say that I won't help Bhimarayya, our friendship will be destroyed. What can I gain by losing this kind of friendship? I will never find such a friend again. I will promise to give my wife to Bhimarayya. Possibly I will find another equally beautiful wife later on."

Somarayya went to his wife and said to her forthrightly, "You must promise not to refuse to do what I say. My friend has fallen completely in love with you, so without argument, you must make love to him tonight."

Somarayya's wife thought, "How can I leave such a husband and go and love some other man? God, you have forsaken me. My virtue has been lost to someone else today. If I disobey my husband, it will be a great sin."

Somarayya and his wife placed four lamps around their bed. They prepared a platter of betel leaves and perfumed areca nut. Somarayya went to the side door of his house and called to Bhimarayya. Bhimarayya entered, laughing and joyous. Somarayya showed him the house of his "female friend" and then went out onto the veranda.

Bhimarayya was astonished by the splendid decoration of the house, by the excellent bedding and by the lamps placed around the bed. He looked in all four directions and sat down happily on the bed.

Bhimarayya called to Somarayya's wife and asked her to adjust the wick of one of the lamps. She adjusted the wick with her finger and wiped the oil from her finger with a cloth. This action convinced Bhimarayya that she was a virtuous woman and he said to her, "Whose wife are you, swear by the sun which shines above. Somarayya told me a lie saying that you were a prostitute, but you are not a prostitute, you are a virtuous woman."

Bhimarayya looked around the house and saw a sword hanging from the wall. He said, "This is Somarayya's sword, this is Somarayya's house, and she is the wife of Somarayya. What a great mistake I have made. How can I show my face to my friend when I get up in the morning?"

Bhimarayya took the sword out of its scabbard, cut his throat and died. Seeing this, Somarayya's wife thought, "If my husband comes and sees the dead body, he will kill me. It is better to die right now." She took the sword and killed herself.

God showed no mercy to the two dead persons. In the morning, Somarayya got up and saw the two corpses. "What a bad thing has happened to me," he thought, "Bhimarayya gave up my friendship and has gone away; with whom can I argue now? And my wife, who was always helping me, where can I find such a wife? When such great souls desert me, what will happen to me?" He picked up the sword and was about to kill himself when Shiva and his wife, Parvati, came and took all three persons to heaven.

Although friends in Gopalpur are not quite as loyal and dutiful as Somarayya and Bhimarayya, the relationships between them are close and important. Friends lend each other equipment and money. They work in each other's fields and, when they need money, they work together for the same landlord. Friends give each other advice and support each other in adversity. When quarrels or interpersonal difficulties develop within a family or within a jati, it is those friends who are not kinsmen who contribute most to the resolution of the dispute.

The larger clique groups, containing a number of pairs of "best friends," come together every evening, and every afternoon when it is too hot to work. To some extent, the clique groups comprise men of roughly the same age living in a particular neighborhood. The Stoneworker men, all of whom live in the same neighborhood and belong to the same lineage, tend to choose their friends from their own family and neighborhood. At the same time, many Stoneworkers have friends in other jatis. Another neighborhood consists largely of Farmers. The remaining two neighborhoods in the village are composed of a number of different jatis. Both neighborhoods and clique groups are vaguely defined and informal in character. The principal differences between them are that neighborhoods are more sharply defined territorially, and cooperation within the neighborhood tends to be between families as a whole rather than between individuals.

Clique groups tend to involve fewer individuals, to contain people of the same age, and to be relatively free of territorial connections. When there are major conflicts within the village, clique groups and neighborhoods come together to form larger parties ("paratis"). Gopalpur has two such factions. Because parties are in conflict with each other, their membership is more sharply defined than is that of clique or neighborhood groupings.

Lineages, jatis, clique groups, and neighborhoods are regarded as desirable by people in Gopalpur; parties are considered to be a symptom of social disorder—the village divided against itself. The emergence of parties is in some ways a direct result of the individual's constant striving for ways and means of increasing the number of kinsmen and friends upon whom he can call in an emergency. Inevitably there comes a time when two men or two families are engaged in direct competition to secure the favor of kinsmen or to attract the support of friends. Families within the village are in direct economic competition with each other because nearly all own land and nearly all wish to own more land, and they are in direct social competition with each other because all seek to multiply alliances within the same pool of potential friends and kinsmen.

The individual in Gopalpur, and, beyond the individual, the village itself, is caught in a web of conflicting needs and allegiances. Within the lineage men compete for brides, within the village jatis compete for position, within the neighborhood men compete for wealth. On a larger scale, villages compete with villages for desirable marriages, for economic relationships, and for favors from the government. The leader, the man with many friends and many active relatives, moves carefully, making alliances and winning people to his side through conspicuous generosity. When a mistake is made, a wife beaten or a friend insulted, the delicate balance of alliances and counteralliances is upset. The result is conflict. Cooperation within the village or between relatives comes to a halt. Such interruptions in the normal course of daily life call into play well-defined mechanisms that restore the balance and bring an end to conflict. These mechanisms, as well as a general explanation for the social system of the village, are to be found in the values, beliefs and ceremonies that constitute the religion of Gopalpur.

5

Religion

Basic Questions

NEAR THE HANUMANTHA GODHOUSE stands the shop operated by Dukhandar. The shop is a rickety lean-to with a shaded veranda in front of it. Inside, Dukhandar's wife sits beside a cupboard containing dozens of tiny drawers filled with condiments and cosmetics. Beside her are sacks of grain, lumps of brown sugar, and the all-important scales. The leaders of one of the "parties" in the village assemble on the veranda. Lesser men sit outside in the darkness under the stars. Dukhandar is a Saltmaker, Tippanna and Hanumantha are Shepherds Big and Little Bhimsha are Farmers. On New Year's night, these men are sitting on the veranda drinking tea, prepared, as usual, by Tippanna. They are waiting for members of the opposing party to finish their private ceremonies in honor of Mariamma. The ceremonies are being held across the road in the Stoneworker's section of the village. The group sitting in front of Dukhandar's shop will wait for a long time; the other party is trying to provoke them into starting a quarrel.

Hanumantha is talking. Once he went to the Bhimsha River and wandered along the beach, collecting pretty stones for his grandson. He looked up and saw a man standing on the opposite side of the river. The man was shouting at him, "The water is coming, the water is coming." Hanumantha scrambled up the steep bank of the river. Before he could get a cigarette out of his pocket, a flash flood swept through the gorge. Everyone agrees that the banks of the Bhima are a dangerous place to be.

Big Bhimsha addresses Dukhandar, "You know, Tippanna is such a man that if anyone gives him a cigarette or something to eat, he talks in favor of that person." Tippanna, thus rewarded for his generous efforts in preparing tea, replies, "Bhimsha is such a small dark person that you can't see him in the night time unless he happens to laugh." Encouraged by the success of his counter attack on Bhimsha, Tippanna turns to the Strangers, "You great people have come to our village, you must do some great service for our village before you leave. We are poor and our village is also poor." Dukhandar answers, "What have they come to do? They have come to study the agriculture of this village. They have nothing. Congress leaders, whom we elected, will have to do all of these things." Tippanna's classificatory son, Hanumantha, speaks, "Yes, they must do all of these things. They have secured our votes by promising that they would do this and that, but they have done nothing." Dukhandar says, "The government has done well by you. It has built roads, schools, and meeting halls, but no man is sending his children to the schools. It is our fault." Big Bhimsha speaks up, "Nobody can do anything except Brahma. What Brahma has written as our fate we must follow. See these big men, they are eating rice and butter every day. We are working day and night, but we don't get even one piece of bread. Brahma has written one kind of fate for us and another kind of fate for them. Nobody can change it, it all depends upon one's fortune."

Little Bhimsha, until then silent in the company of his elders, interrupts, "Where is this Brahma? Is he going to write everyone's fate until his death? Is he going to watch everyone's life? That is all wrong, the man who works hard will succeed in this life." Hanumantha and Little Bhimsha begin to argue. Hanumantha loses his temper and says, "When big people are talking, you have to be careful. You should not say one after another every word that comes into your head." Little Bhimsha subsides. The men seated in front of the store go in procession to the godhouses of the village. They sit in front of the store and accompany the Singer while he sings praises of the various gods.

The next day is New Year's day and the Astrologer and other Brahmins living nearby gather in front of the Hanumantha godhouse. So important is the occasion that even the Accountant and the Gauda are present. The Astrologer begins to read in Sanskirt concerning Brahma's one hundred years of life and the length of each of those years. The assembled crowd understands little of what is being read, but it is obvious that time stretches infinitely into the past and infinitely into the future. The Astrologer reads the year, the age, and the cycle, giving the appropriate name of each. The mathematical preamble completed, the Astrologer reads:

In this year, Brahma will not take complete care of the crops. The cold season crops will be better than the rainy season crops. There will be many difficulties encountered by the officials of government. The people will suffer greatly from disease. There will be much rain this year. Cows will give much milk. The people will perform ceremonies and sacrifices well this year. As a result, in this world all will be happy. In this year, everything is good. Those who are named Hanumantha will be fortunate.

Gods and their works are a continuous part of present reality in Gopalpur. Gods attend and take part in almost every ceremony. Sometimes a priest, sometimes even a perfectly ordinary person like Hanumantha, begins to tremble. His arms shake uncontrollably; his legs move violently in response to the drumming. Sometimes the affected person screams and falls to the ground. The face goes rigid. Suddenly, the body is still and the voice of one of the gods speaks through his mouth. The god may make predictions, answer questions, or give orders concerning the manner in which a particular ceremony is to be conducted.

Kinds of Gods

The order of gods is, in many ways, parallel to the order of men. There are high gods, bearing such names as Shiva, Vishnu, Rama, Basava, Gopal, Hanumantha, and Bhimarayya, who are worshipped by vegetarian priests. These gods, connected with the higher-ranking jatis, are generally beneficent. Hanumantha and Bhimarayya are specifically charged with protecting villages, arranging successful marriages, and ensuring that married couples bear children. In a general way, these gods resemble the higher-ranking government officials. They are generally kindly, but it is difficult to obtain an interview with them. One must deal with the vegetarian priests who themselves must be familiar with the rituals and the sacred verses essential to an approach to such deities. Proper worship of the high gods is likely to be expensive and, even then, may not produce proportionate results. With a few exceptions, worship of the high gods in Gopalpur is confined to the Brahmin Gauda and to the Jangama priest brought to the village by the Gauda.

Because Hanumantha and Bhimarayya, two forms of the same god, are especially partial to the people of the Gopalpur region, they may be worshipped with comparative ease. As high gods go, Hanumantha and Bhimarayya are unsophisticated and rough. They are essentially warrior gods unconcerned with ritual niceties. Even so, only a Brahmin dares to touch their images. Another high god worshipped in Gopalpur is Shah Hussein, "the god of the Turks." Shah Hussein differs from other high gods in that he accepts offerings of meat and is worshipped by a nonvegetarian priesthood. His sacred ritual is conducted in the Urdu language rather than in Sanskirt. Hanumantha and Shah Hussein are Gopalpur's special gods. They stand ready to help in any emergency, but their assistance is always conditional upon the good behavior of people in Gopalpur. In one of his appearances during 1959, Hanumantha had this to say, "If you don't worship with a good heart, you will be burned to ashes." Shah Hussein, speaking in Urdu, puts it more subtly, "Worship me when you feel happy." Worship of the high gods requires that all members of the community participate, and that their manner be joyful and friendly. At such times, the quarrels between the two parties are forgotten, and no one is turned away from any man's door with an empty stomach.

Below the male gods are nonvegetarian goddesses. The function of these goddesses is to protect the village from particular disasters, from flood and smallpox, from cholera and skin disease. When people are sinful, failing to perform appropriate sacrifices or violating the moral code, one of the goddesses approaches God and asks permission to punish the village—"The mother punishes the child after getting the father's permission." If there is an epidemic of smallpox or cholera, the village is purified, and offerings are made to an appropriate goddess. The priests of the goddesses are drawn from the lower-ranking jatis; they need not be paid much money. The expense of worshipping a goddess stems from the fact that a goddess is not to be satisfied with vegetarian offerings, but must have meat and beer. Some goddesses, such as Mariamma, the goddess of cholera, and Pollamma, the goddess of smallpox, serve the entire village. They, along with Hanumantha and Shah Hussein, are worshipped on all holy days. Other goddesses inhabit fields belonging to particular individuals. These goddesses are appeased at harvest time if the crops are good. Often, when there is sickness in the family, an appeal is made to one of the gods or goddesses. If the sick person recovers, offerings are made to the deity considered responsible. In general, the attitude of people in Gopalpur toward goddesses and minor gods is one of strict reciprocity.

There is no sharp line of demarcation between gods, men, and animals. All are part of the single unity described as "God," "Brahma," or "Paramahatma." God is all-inclusive as well as all-powerful and all-knowing. When a man dies, God consults his records and determines whether the dead man has spent his life helping or injuring others. Those who have done bad things to others are sent to the Underworld, where they suffer hideous tortures. They are later reborn in the stomachs of dogs, donkeys, or worms. People who lead good lives are reborn as men. If their previous lives were very good, they become great kings and sit on thrones. A really perfect man can be considered to be an earthly reincarnation of one of the gods. Not only are Hanumantha and Bhimarayya representations of different earthly experiences of the same god, but people named Hanumantha and Bhimarayya may come to be considered in some way manifestations of the gods Hanumantha and Bhimarayya. It is for this reason that most parents in Gopalpur name their male children, Hanumantha, Bhimarayya, or Saba (referring to Shah Hussein).

Different godhouses and holy places have different stories attached to them, for each is linked to a different manifestation of the gods they are devoted to. Shah Hussein of Gopalpur appears to have died in the village within living memory. He was a saintly man, and after his death he agreed to stay in the village and protect it. What is worshipped is the tomb of a particular man, but it is worshipped as if the man were, in fact, the god. The same is true of Gopalpur Mariamma, the smallpox goddess. She was a Stoneworker who, long ago, married a man from the neighboring village. Her spirit resides in the Stoneworker's section of the village and makes annual journeys to visit her husband. She is worshipped as if she were the smallpox goddess, but she is not identical with the smallpox goddesses in other villages, and the stories told about her origin and character are somewhat different from those told concerning other forms of Mariamma.

Sometimes, although evidently not within living memory, an individual dies without completing the things that were to be accomplished during his life on earth, or perhaps it is that an individual dies still hungry for sex, or food, or some other gratification. When this happens, the individual is likely to return from his or her grave and attack living people. Such attacks are most frequently made upon those who go outside in the dark of the moon without carrying a lantern. Although there have been no recent attacks, it is said that the spirits enter into living men and cause them to behave in strange ways. When such things happen, the victim is beaten with a whip or with sandals until the spirit becomes uncomfortable and promises to leave. Sometimes the departure of the spirit is accelerated by offering him a chicken or a goat.

Sin and Virtue

With the possible exception of these attacks by ghosts and spirits, which occur rarely if at all, everything that happens to a man is determined by his behavior in his former life as well as by his behavior in his present life. One's birth as a god or man or animal is determined by one's behavior. One's level of birth as a man is also determined by one's behavior. The fact that one is born as a high man or a low man entitles one to the rights and privileges deriving from one's birth, but it also imposes upon one the duties inherent in one's station in life. The king may be a bad king or a good king; his subjects owe him obedience regardless of his personal qualities.

There is a definite connection between sin, and ritual or ceremonial purity. It might be said that sins are the actions which lead one away from purity and, hence, away from any ultimate merger with the basic oneness that is God. Virtuous actions are those which contribute to the harmonious functioning of the social order and of the universe. Virtuous actions lead toward oneness. On this showing, it is clear that competition and conflict within the village is sinful. Nevertheless, much of the activity taking place within the village is an expression of competition and conflict.

Surely, even if the people in Gopalpur cannot arrive at an appropriate definition of sin, it should be possible for the priests and philosophers, who articulate the higher religious thought of the region, to formulate a logically consistent description of sin and virtue. The difficulty appears to lie in the fact that the concept of levels of purity and of virtue within society is used to support the system of ranked jatis. Logically, only those born into the highest jatis are actually capable of leading their lives without committing sins. Consider the Stoneworker who sacrifices a goat to the cholera goddess. Is his action virtuous or sinful? The Stoneworker is required to make such sacrifices by virtue of the fact that he was born into a jati whose duty it is to make sacrifices. Why does God create a nonvegetarian jati if he does not expect it to consume meat? It is not clear whether it is a greater sin to disobey God directly by refusing to make sacrifices, or to make sacrifices and take life.

Virtue, in the absolute sense, consists of absolute conformity to the highest moral code; virtue, in the relative sense, consists of absolute conformity to the rules governing one's station in life. The conflict between these two kinds of virtue is expressed in Gopalpur through reference to Kali Yuga and *samsara,* the buzzing, blooming confusion. Kali Yuga, the current age, is vaguely defined in Gopalpur. Essentially, it is an age when nothing goes right and when the actions of all are sinful. Samsara refers to family life and, in a more refined sense, to the ocean of confusing impressions and observations encountered by anyone who attempts to come to terms with reality.

Everyone in Gopalpur is aware that there is a way to avoid committing sins and to avoid the unfortunate consequences of being born in this age of misery and mismanagement. The way out consists of foregoing all earthly desires and becoming an ascetic. An ascetic is required to abandon his family, to live on fruits and milk, and to wander from place to place. Nowadays, "There are a few persons known as ascestics. They are filled to the brim with bad habits. They say bad things, they carry on family life, and they eat rice. They are all fake ascetics." People can understand how an old man or some other person who is free of responsibilities towards others might legitimately become an ascetic. They have nothing but contempt for a man who leaves his family and jettisons his responsibilities in order to save himself. In a sense, it is considered far more virtuous to do whatever needs to be done to guarantee the support of one's wife and children, than to lead a life free of sin or desire. The role of ascetic is a coward's role. The head of a family, even though he must lie, cheat, or steal, provides for his dependents and gives them the opportunity for favorable future rebirth.

Nearly everyone in Gopalpur accepts the proposition that he must maintain virtuous behavior in accordance with his station in life. What this involves is explained in one of the songs recited by the Singer:

> Set aside Passion and Anger,
> Put away Recklessness, Jealousy,
> Completely incinerate Greed.
> Blot out Vanity and Pride.
> Avoid the forms of Evil,
> Eliminate evil thoughts.
> Never criticize one another,
> Never say "I" and "You."
> Worship God in the fullness of wisdom.
>
> Come and go with men who are moral,
> Follow the path of Goodness.
> Serve all teachers and elders,
> Bow down before holy men.
> Care for fathers and mothers
> Visit kith and kin,
> Leave sin and practice virtue.
> Worship God in the fullness of wisdom.
>
> Make a light in the darkness,
> Marry a woman who is wise,
> Sleep with your wife at midnight,
> Rise at dawn singing God's praises.
> Punish neighbors who do evil,
> Sit in public to settle disputes.
> Sift the evidence slowly,

When righteously angry move slowly.
Worship God in the fullness of wisdom.

Act boldly against enemies,
Divide fairly among brothers.
Take account of profit in your business.
Take the pulse when practicing medicine.
Eat meals at the proper time,
Know the relationship before arranging a marriage.
Face poverty carrying on boldly,
Plow the fragment of farmland.
Eat one meal daily from full moon to new moon.
Worship God in the fullness of wisdom.

Offer rice to those who are hungry,
Use God's gifts to perform good deeds.
Love men from other countries.
Understand the six great rule books,
Memorize the eighteen great stories,
Think about the four great scriptures.
Have strength of will,
Roof the house of your spirit,
Care for the doors of your body.
Worship God in the fullness of wisdom.

Guard your wealth and increase it,
Count your money every week.
Ask the day and worship God accordingly,
Obey the words of holy men.
Study character before making friends,
Journey to the fair with your companions,
Form friendships in every village.
Camp for the night an hour before sunset,
Remember death every day.
Worship God in the fullness of wisdom.

Pray to Rama and Bhima,
Worship, do penance, recite sacred verses.
Return what has been borrowed,
Travel to the Holy City,
Make verses with alliteration.
Straighten out your lies and faults,
Keep your promises.
Turn your faces to the Great Ones,
Bless whoever stands before you.
Worship God in the fullness of wisdom.

A bitter holy man in one of the villages of the region has written another song, "Right Action in the Age of Kali."

In the old days, just like priests,
Our grandmother was afraid of our father and our father's father.
Our ancestors, so we are told, came to the teacher
Trembling, with shaking legs and bowed heads.
In this Age, Sin has come and wrapped itself around our necks.

Now, the mother-in-law has become a dependent of the daughter-in-law;
The son is quarreling with his father.
The younger brother visits the older brother's wife;
The older brother goes to fetch his sister and sins on the way home.

The husband is afraid of his second wife;
The father is afraid of his son;
The Gauda is afraid of low-caste people;
Truthteller is afraid of us all.
The teacher is frightened and sits in the corner.

The average man in Gopalpur considers himself, his close friends, and his relatives, to be virtuous in conformity with the principles given in the first song; most other people in the village are considered to be nonvirtuous in conformity with the second song. A good man feeds his family well and gives help to all who ask for help. If a woman leaves her husband, the good man advises her to return; if there is a quarrel, the good man gives sage advice and makes peace. A bad man cuts grain in other people's fields, steals money, starts quarrels, and "spoils" other men's wives. As a matter of fact, the average man has stolen grain from other men's fields, and has quarreled with his neighbors. There is a strong possibility that he has also stolen money or property, or slept with his neighbor's wife. The average man does not consider his own actions to constitute violations of the moral code. He did those things in order to punish neighbors who failed to conform to the code. The average man's actions conform to the directive, "Punish neighbors who do evil."

Choosing Right Actions

There is no generally accepted hierarchy of moral imperatives. One should obey one's teacher, one's Gauda and one's parents. No one knows what to do if these three figures give conflicting orders. If the present age were not the Age of Kali, teachers, Gaudas, and parents would be in agreement. The hard fact is that they are not. The moral problem of choosing between two equally correct alternatives is the basic plot of almost every song or story sung or told in Gopalpur. Should Lakshmi marry the man her father chooses, or should she run away? What should Somarayya do for his friend Bhimarayya? In the "Railroad Conductor Song," a woman's father is dilatory in returning her to her husband when the latter comes to fetch her. Should she obey her father, or her husband? She decides to go with her husband, and runs to the railway station. The train has left. The conductor asks her to spend the night in an elegant waiting room. She agrees, only to discover that the conductor plans to seduce her. She locks the conductor in the waiting room with her baby. The conductor threatens to kill the baby unless she unlocks the door. She waits outside while the conductor tears the baby to pieces and throws the pieces through the window. She says to herself, "I can always have another child; I can never recover my virtue once it is lost."

There are many choices. A man can feed his family or be generous to all. He can obey the Gauda or his father. He can care for his children or for his younger brother. He can guard his wealth and cause it to increase, or he can use his profits to perform good deeds. He can smite his enemies or avoid angry and quarrelsome behavior. Many men dream of giving up samsara, this confusion of wordly things, and of becoming ascetics. They look at their wives and children and are unable to leave the village.

The average man is painfully conscious of his own virtue. Often, when asked to describe a virtuous man, he can do no better than to describe himself. At the same time, he is aware that there are a great many people who question his virtue. There are people who consider him to be stingy or dishonest or quarrelsome. Probably, the average man worries a great deal about his own virtue. His behavior is consistent with the notion that he lacks the security of any inner conviction of righteousness.

The Arbitrator

The average man's image of the Gauda, the Village Headman, is of a man who is wise and admirable, in every way superior to ordinary men. The Gauda, himself, the superior man who is wealthier and better educated than anyone else, is an essential part of the social order. A good Gauda is a man who is fair, a man who arbitrates disputes, a man who sets fire to evil doers. The "strength" of a Gauda is derived neither from force of arms nor from land ownership. It is derived from the fact that the Gauda is, by definition, wise enough and good enough to thread the difficult path between conflicting values. By investing the Gauda with superhuman abilities and attaching to his role the sacred function of separating right action and wrong action, the individual in Gopalpur relieves himself of ultimate responsibilities for his own actions.

Another way in which the individual deals with the problem of his own goodness or badness is through concrete actions that have the effect of wiping out accumulated sin, and that demonstrate good intentions. A man expresses his virtue by giving gifts of food to the gods and by sharing the leftovers with other men. The sharing of food among gods, friends, neighbors, and kinsmen is an act in which childhood training, economics, social life, and religion intersect.

As a personality, it is probable that an individual relieves his fears of supernatural punishment through self-deprivation or sacrifice. As a social being, by such acts the individual is compelling others to admit his superiority, his fellowship, and his control over them. The meaning attached to food and to the giving of food is firmly established in early childhood, when the mother uses food as a means of controlling her child. In childhood, food and love are exchanged for work and obedience. In later life, the individual learns that a gift must always be returned, if not in this life, then in a later life. When a man gives food to a beggar, he establishes his superiority, he relieves himself of sin, and he demonstrates himself to be a virtuous man. He is virtuous precisely because he has something to give—the reward for virtue in former lives is success in this life. The compelling impact of food gifts upon others applies to gods as well as to men. Gifts from a god are repaid through sacrifice. Sacrifice compels a god to make a suitable return. When rains fail, men say, "We perform his ceremonies well, but God has cheated us."

The Ceremonies

The major form of religious activity in Gopalpur is the religious ceremony in which men make gifts of food to the gods and, as a consequence, make gifts of food to other men. At a ceremony, the hosts receive open acknowledgement that they are recognized members of the social system. By the act of taking his food, the guest admits acceptance of the host. The guest also acquires thereby an obligation to his host. In view of the parallels between the order of gods and the order of men, and the basic, harmonious oneness of the universe, it follows that the harmonious congregation of men in ceremonial activities is a precondition for the harmonious functioning of the universe. Ceremonies express harmony among villages, harmony among relatives, harmony among friends and neighbors, and harmony within the family. Without such harmony, there can be no ceremony. Without a ceremony, there can be no divine support of human endeavor.

In the fair or *jatra,* one village plays host to a set of neighboring villages. For the host village, the holding of its annual fair is a ritual necessity. The Gopalpur fair expresses the satisfaction of the people of Gopalpur with the manner in which Shah Hussein has protected the village. If the fair is not held, there is every likelihood that the supernatural protection of Shah Hussein will be withdrawn. If the fair is to be held at all, every family in Gopalpur must contribute to the holding of the ceremony. Even the Gauda, who, as a vegetarian, cannot attend the ceremony, provides the land upon which it is held. Equally, the fair cannot be held unless people from neighboring villages are prepared to play the role of guest. The active or public expression of conflict within Gopalpur, or between Gopalpur and the invited villages, renders holding of the fair impossible.

The fair permits several kinds of regulated competition. While members of the host village serve as referees, young men from neighboring villages participate in wrestling matches as representatives of their villages. The act of holding a fair is an expression of competition between the host village and neighboring villages, for each village attempts to produce the "best" fair. Designed, in a sense, as an expression of goodwill and friendliness towards all, fairs are frequently the scene of violent rioting, usually connected with the wrestling matches. The fair provides a temporary cessation of conflict, but it also provides a time, a place, and because weapons cannot be brought to a fair, a limitation on the choice of weapons used in conflict between villages. The young man seeking to become a hero displays his strength on the wrestling ground; any other form of conflict with neighboring villages becomes an expression of bad sportsmanship, not of heroism. Controlled conflict between villages, expressed in the fair, permits free travel throughout the region, and the carrying on of economic and social exchange between villages.

Almost every twenty-eight days, a month based on the lunar calendar, there is a calendrical ceremony in Gopalpur. Every housewife acquires stores of wheat flour and brown sugar, and sets about the manufacture of festival delicacies. Other members of the family capture friends and relatives and compel them to partake of the family feast. Those who appear in the doorway during the day must enter and eat before they are permitted to go about their business. If a "mother's brother" or other important person comes, the six-year-old scurries off to the store to buy expensive paper-wrapped cigarettes and specially flavored areca nut. The calendrical ceremony is always a village-wide ceremony. Everyone participates, everyone strives to exhibit the holiday spirit of cooperation, friendliness, and generosity. Throughout the day, families make offerings to the gods of their house and to the various gods of the village. Sometimes during the day, more often after dark, the entire village marches in procession. A coconut is broken at the stone in the center of the village representing the village gate. The entire procession then goes before the Gauda's house, and then through the village, visiting every godhouse. Finally, the procession reaches the Hanumantha godhouse where more coconuts are broken, and puffed rice mixed with brown sugar and coconut is distributed among everyone present.

Representatives of virtually every jati in Gopalpur have a special role to play in each of the calendrical ceremonies. All must cooperate if the crops are to be good, and if the life of the village is to be happy. Sisters and daughters, the women whose daughters are "potential wives" of men in Gopalpur, are invited to the more important calendrical ceremonies. Every effort is made to remind them that Gopalpur is a happy village. The calendrical ceremony is a break in the routine; it is a time-marker, signalling the change of seasons; it is a mode of advertising the good qualities of a particular village; it is a way of appealing to the gods for continued favor.

The calendrical ceremony is also a means of expressing discontent. Relatives may refuse to visit. The Priest or Barber, the Shepherd or Farmer, may refuse to participate. Grievances are brought into the open. The father must go to his daughter's husband and ask, "Why will you not give me my daughter?" The daughter's husband then explains, "Before the wedding you promised to give two silver leg chains. At the time of the wedding you said that you would give the chains later. Five years have passed and the silver leg chains have not appeared." Important men, who witnessed the wedding, gather. The father promises to purchase leg chains (a promise that may well be forgotten), and accompanies his daughter to Gopalpur. When the Priest or Barber or some other person in Gopalpur refuses to perform his appointed role in a calendrical ceremony, arbitration again takes place.

When arbitration fails, ceremonies may be disrupted by violent conflict. The ceremony ends before it has been completed despite the fact that this is certain to bring down the anger of the gods. After the conflict, the "mother's brothers" come to Gopalpur. Impressive men, with white whiskers and silk turbans, the "mother's brothers" lecture their relatives, "Are there nothing but gangsters in your village?" When men from Gopalpur go to the landlord of the neighboring village to borrow grain for their sowing, the landlord refuses. A village in conflict is a bad risk because people will steal each other's grain. Even the bully, who runs like a mad dog through the streets of a village inflicting injury on any man who stands in his way, has a family and must therefore obey his "mother's brother." Even the bully must borrow seed and must therefore obey his creditor.

Almost every day, particularly during the hot season, some family in Gopalpur is giving a name to a child, negotiating a marriage, celebrating a marriage, holding a girl's puberty ceremony, or conducting the feast that follows a funeral. At the time such rites of passage are held, the family must muster up its supporting group of kinsmen, and make use of the services of other jatis in the village. If a householder has quarreled with his relatives, or has failed in his commitments to the Barber, the Blacksmith, or the Priest, he must make peace before his child can receive a name, before his younger brother can be married, before his daughter can establish a sexual relationship with her husband, before his father can go to his grave or, later, to heaven. Rites of passage announce a change in the status of an individual and of his family; they secure supernatural approval of the change of status; and they secure approval of the village and of the leaders of the village. Although any ceremony may serve as an excuse for the entertainment of relatives, the rite of passage is the primary means of preserving and developing the status of the individual family within the circle of kin. The wedding ceremonies, probably because they involve the activation of latent relationships through the exchange of personnel between two families and two villages, are the most complicated and dramatic of the rites of passage.

Crisis ceremonies, held at times of drought or epidemic and participated in by the entire village, are the most purely religious of the religious ceremonies, their purpose being largely confined to appeasement of the deities. The fact that the entire village is enabled to engage in direct action to counter the threat of drought or epidemic serves to reaffirm the value of the village organization as a cooperative unit, and to prevent panic or the abandonment of hope. Such ceremonies and such crises occur relatively rarely, perhaps once in five years.

Parallel ceremonies dealing with the crises of individual families are comparatively frequent, but they are not notably different from ceremonies designed to overcome communal crises. A family may hold a ceremony, for example, when the head of the family is ill. Or the family may promise to hold a ceremony when the head of the family recovers and the crisis is over. In either case, the pattern is essentially the same. A goat or sheep is purchased and given to an eight- or nine-year-old child, or to an old man if there is no child. The caretaker of the goat devotes his time to the fattening and grooming of the sacrificial animal. When the animal is ready, friends, neighbors, and kinsmen are invited and all go in procession past the godhouses of the village, out to the fields where a family shrine is located. Offerings are made to the particular god or goddess to whom the family shrine is sacred, the goat is sacrificed, and the women set about boiling meat and rice. While the women cook, men sit in a circle around a fire and sing hymns. The hymn singing is led by the Singer. Because the crisis generally has passed by the time such a family ceremony is held, the ceremony becomes a celebration, and one of its major functions becomes that of entertainment. This is particularly true when the ceremony takes place after a successful harvest.

From one viewpoint, the family crisis ceremony is a gay party given for the nightlong entertainment of the family and the friends of the family. People in Gopalpur are avid partygoers and partygivers. Such parties are the principal mechanism used by the individual family to increase its status within the community and to develop a circle of friends and supporters. The successful man justifies his elevation to a superior position by sharing his wealth with others. Because he has many things to be thankful for, he tends to hold ceremonies frequently. Operating in terms of goodwill from both god and man, the successful man is fortunate. His daughter marries well, his fields are not robbed, and his cattle are not beaten when they invade the fields of others.

Not everyone can be invited to the party, and not everyone can give parties at the same time. Only a very successful man, a Gauda, can afford to feed all comers. As a family head attempts to build social support through generosity, he inevitably runs afoul of his own inability to be equally a friend of all. The desire to build alliances and to develop a circle of supporters conflicts with other men's desires to do the same thing. Not every man can "make his name great," and when one man succeeds in doing so, other men band together in opposition to him. Where the Gauda provides weak or ineffective leadership, or where there is more than one "big man" in a village, the search for security and support through the giving of ceremonies leads inevitably to insecurity and conflict.

In Gopalpur, gods and men strive for harmony and work toward a peaceful, happy world where there is no sin. The individual man attempts to extend ever outward his circle of kinsmen and his circle of friends. Bonds of territoriality and of common descent are stretched to include the villages of an entire region and to develop a common set of concepts and ways of acting affecting millions of people. Inevitably these bonds, stretched out across many miles and affecting many people, snap. It is the task of the gods and the gaudas to restore order.

6

Patterns of Action

The Rules

GOPALPUR is a cluster of gray houses, a tree-covered island in the center of a dusty, featureless plain. More than this, Gopalpur is an aggregate of people who follow a particular set of rules of life, which might be described as the structure of Gopalpur. They are derived from the shape of the village itself, from the kinds of houses people live in, from the presence or absence of rain, from the kinds of things a man must do in order to grow crops. The rules of life are derived also from the early experience of the child and the manner in which it is brought into acceptable conformity with these rules. They are, moreover, expressed in the relationships among relatives, and in the relationships between jatis, and among neighbors. Finally, their idealized expression is summarized in the beliefs, values, and ritual activities of Gopalpur's religious life.

The individual operates within the rules handed down from his fore-fathers, which have been formulated by the interaction of Gopalpur with the men, animals, things, and forces surrounding it. In some ways, there is a re-semblance to the rules of a game. It is helpful to know the rules, but knowing them alone does not make one a skilled player. To understand a game, it is necessary to understand the choices or strategies available to each of the players. To understand Gopalpur, it is necessary to know how different individuals adapt to the circumstances in which they find themselves, and how they behave when their life strategies cross and become entangled in conflict. Consider, first, the background and style of the Gauda's life.

The Gauda

Four miles south of Gopalpur is the village of Totlur. At present, nearly all the lands in Totlur, over 800 acres, are owned by an absentee landlord. Tenants who farm the landlord's fields cannot afford to fertilize them. Every year, the fields yield less; every year, more people leave to search for jobs in Bombay, Surat, and Ahmedabad. On the northern side of Totlur stands a great stone house. The roof beams have rotted and the doors have fallen so that visitors can look through the doorways at the rubble and desolation within. According to people in Gopalpur, the Gauda's grandfather once lived in the ruined house, and ruled seventeen villages. Daily he rode his horse through the villages under his control, punishing immodest women, and chastising those who quarreled or misbehaved.

The landlords of Yelher, the village standing between Gopalpur and Totlur, and the government officials in Yadgiri were afraid of the Gauda's grandfather, so the story goes, and endlessly plotted his destruction. On one occasion, forty armed men surrounded the grandfather as he was riding his horse along a dark and desolate pathway. He turned his horse and escaped by jumping across one of the great wells used for irrigation. One day, a servant attempted to ride the horse and was killed when it ran under a tree. The grandfather was accused of murder and the police came to arrest him. As the police waited outside the door, the grandfather took poison and died.

The Gauda's father was the same kind of man, riding tirelessly through his villages, righting wrongs and enforcing virtue. A government official who had been taking bribes was offered a large sum of money by the Gauda's father. The government official came to the house during the night. He received the money and walked out of the door into the arms of waiting police officials. Everyone was afraid of the Gauda's father. People trembled when he addressed them, and no one in any of the villages under his control dared step out of line.

The old men in Gopalpur tell many tales of the Gauda's father and grandfather; when they have finished, they shake their heads sadly. Such men are no longer to be found. The fortunes of the Gauda's family have dwindled. The great ceremonies at which people from many villages were fed are no longer held. The Gauda no longer possesses great stores of grain and no longer distributes vast quantities of cloth. Nowadays, people are turned away from the Gauda's house when they ask for jobs or loans of grain and money. Many men borrow from the Lingayat and Reddi landlords of neighboring villages. The Gauda is active in politics and has had to establish a household in Yadgiri, where he lives for a good part of the year. The Gauda's wife is unhappy in Gopalpur, and presses continually for opportunities to return to the town where there are electric lights, running water, and people worth talking to.

Even though, if the old people are correct, the present Gauda is not as magnificent as his father and grandfather were, very few people in Gopalpur will criticize the Gauda. Sometimes, a man recently returned from the city will grumble, and even hint at open revolt. For the most part, everyone is delighted at opportunities to serve the Gauda. When they pass his house and see him seated on the veranda, they bow low and touch their hands reverently to their foreheads. If the Gauda wants his mail delivered from the neighboring village, someone is ready to fetch it. If the Gauda wants cigarettes from the store, someone will bring them. When a man's field is robbed, he goes to the Gauda's house to complain. If a man's wife runs away, he reports to the Gauda. If the

Gauda wants a husky young man to work in his fields, he has but to ask the boy's father. From time to time, there is grumbling. The Gauda is stingy. The Gauda doesn't hold enough ceremonies. He spends too much on his own family. He is too demanding. He does not settle quarrels fairly or quickly. Whatever the Gauda's faults might be, people regard him as the father of the village. He may not be a great warrior, he may not be a great giver of feasts, but he is a Brahmin and an educated man. He is "our Gauda."

To the sophisticated government officials in Yadgiri, and even to the progressive landlords of some of the neighboring villages, Gopalpur's Gauda seems to be a quaint survival of a former age. The *Tahsildar* (head of Tahsil) believes the Gauda to be an oppressor of the poor, a man who mistreats and abuses the people under his care, the kind of man who will disappear when a democratic government has been firmly established, preferably by force, within the region. The day when a man might own a village and the people in it has passed. This dramatic, "class war" interpretation of the role of the Gauda in Gopalpur is that of an outsider. The truth is that the Gauda is the creation of the people in Gopalpur. He exists, because his existence is necessary to the pattern of life in the village. The basic configuration of the Gauda's character is the result of the training given to the Gauda during his childhood by the people of Gopalpur. Consider the Gauda's son:

The Gauda's son is eighteen months old. Every morning, a boy employed by the Gauda carries the Gauda's son through the streets of Gopalpur. When the boy is not available to perform this service, a poor relation brought to Gopalpur for that purpose, carries the child. The Gauda's son is clean; his clothing is elegant. When he is carried along the street, the old woman stop their ceaseless grinding and pounding of grain and gather around. The Carpenter puts down his tools to talk to the Gauda's son. If the child wants something to play with, he is given it. If he cries, there is consternation. If he plays with another boy, watchful adults make sure that the other boy does nothing to annoy the Gauda's son. People ignore their own children to keep painful track of each new word learned by the Gauda's son. Any man who makes a good impression on the Gauda's son will be certain to profit later on.

Shielded by servants, protected and comforted by virtually everyone in the village, the Gauda's son soon learns that tears and rage will produce anything he wants. This is a lesson that he will never forget. At the same time, he begins to learn that the same superiority which gives him license to direct others and to demand their services places him in a state of danger. The green mangoes eaten by all of the other children in the village will give him a fever; coarse and chewy substances are likely to give him a stomach-ache. While other children clothe themselves in mud and dirt, he finds himself constantly being washed. Where other children toilet-train themselves, indifferently, and over a long period, he is early impressed with the fact that his feces and urine are dangerous and defiling. He is toilet trained as soon as possible and his accidents are family crises, horrifying to his father and mother. As a Brahmin, he is taught to avoid all forms of pollution and to carry out complicated daily rituals of bathing, eating, sleeping, and all other normal processes of life.

In time, the Gauda's son will enter school. He will sit motionless for hours, memorizing long passages from Sanskrit holy books and long poems in English and Urdu. He will learn to perform the rituals that are the duty of every Brahmin. He will bathe daily in the cold water of the private family well, reciting prayers and following a strict procedure. The gods in his house are major deities who must be worshipped every day, at length and with great care. When he attends high school and college, it is possible that he will abandon many of the religious rituals practiced by his father and his father's father, but he will continue to spend the hours between dawn and 10:00 a.m. bathing and grooming himself. Gopalpur creates its Gauda because the village has a need for a superior being, one beyond the ordinary. Someone is needed who can deal with the great forces of the world outside the village, with government officials, and with the mysterious higher gods. That the life of the Gauda is one of loneliness, misery, and fear is of little concern to the men and women who gather around his child.

The Gauda rises at dawn. After drinking a cup of tea, he commences his daily bath. Until ten o'clock he conducts his morning worship, after which he eats. A servant carries a faded Persian carpet out to the veranda. On it he places a wooden writing desk containing a pen, an inkwell, and a book the Gauda is currently reading. He sits behind the desk and reads or writes. People passing in the street touch their foreheads, but he is too busy to notice. Sometimes he shouts at a passerby, "Hey, you, where are you going?" The passerby answers and is dismissed with a curt nod. As servants pass in and out of the front door of the house, he shouts instructions at them. He scolds them for beating the cattle. He has scolded them every morning, but they continue to handle the cattle in their own way. The Gauda knows nothing about agriculture. He suspects that when he is not watching, his servants stop work to gossip or sleep. Whenever he sees his servants, he tells them to work harder, longer, and faster. From time to time, one of the more important men in the village comes and sits on the ground in the doorway beneath the platform on which the Gauda sits. The Gauda asks questions and gives instructions. Later, someone may be beaten or a theft may be committed, but the Gauda will not send a report to the police.

During the heat of the afternoon, the Gauda enters his house and sleeps. At 3 o'clock, he again takes his place on his veranda. In the cool of evening, he may demand his horse and ride out into the fields. In one field, he sees a stalk of millet that has been cut. He calls the watchman, shows him the stalk, and demands an explanation. The watchman explains that thieves come in the night to distant parts of the field. The watchman sleeps on a platform in the center of the field. The Gauda advises him to sleep on the ground and occupy a different part of the field each night. In his garden, the Gauda discovers that another watchman has removed tamarind from his tree. It occurs to the Gauda that the fruits of that particular tree should be distributed to everyone in the village. The theft of the fruits is not a crime against himself; it is a crime against the entire village. Perhaps, tomorrow, the watchman will be beaten; perhaps, tomorrow, the Gauda will go to Yadgiri to live for a month or two and the incident will be forgotten.

For years, the Brahmins of the Gopalpur region have suffered under British and Muslim rule. During the long period of the struggle for independence, the words and thought of Mahatma Gandhi and the Congress Party made a deep impression upon the educated people of the region. After the Muslim ruler of Hyderabad had been deposed, the Gauda became an active member of the Congress Party. The simple life advocated by Gandhi appeals to Gopalpur's Gauda. Of course, only a saint could be expected to weave his own cloth or to dispose of his material possessions. The country would not long survive if everyone were to live as Gandhi lived. Although the Gauda dismisses many of the Mahatma's ideas, he heartily endorses Self-Help and Village Self-Government.

In the Gauda's view, the trouble with India is that the ordinary person has become lazy, insolent, and demanding. Instead of working hard, people spend money on weddings and ceremonies. The Gauda himself faces peculiar problems in the modern age. He must send his children to the university in order to prepare them for the government jobs they so earnestly desire. He requires a large income. Since money that is spent upon the education of the Gauda's children cannot be loaned to or used to provide jobs for people in Gopalpur, the Gauda lends relatively little money and holds few ceremonies, "They must help themselves; they must give up spending money on weddings and ceremonies; they must learn to work hard." To the Gauda, Self-Help means that he is no longer required to assist the people of his village. The new age of democracy and self-government has liberated the Gauda from his traditional responsibilities—lending money, feeding people, and giving away clothing.

As a member of the Congress Party, the Gauda is able to interpret the Gandhian concept of Village Self-Government to officials who visit the village. The basis of his concept is that he should rule the village and the officials should stay away. As Headman of the village, he should be permitted to collect taxes as he sees fit. The government should not spoil the people by introducing schools and community development projects. When the Strangers came to Gopalpur, government officials also came; the Tahsildar inspected the village. What if the Strangers should write that there was no school house in the village? The Tahsildar approached the Gauda, explaining that the government would pay the cost of all materials, the people of Gopalpur need only pile the necessary stones on top of one another. All that was needed was a petition addressed to the government.

When the five parents in Gopalpur who send their children to school talked of circulating a petition, the Gauda's assistant, the Police Headman, declared: "No, we don't want any school. No one is willing to send his children to school. The school master is not teaching properly. Most people send their children only during the hot season. The boys are busy during the rainy season, herding buffaloes and bullocks. The government must supply us with grain, and pay us all a monthly salary. If they supply slates, clothing, books, and pencils, we will send our children to school."

The five parents appealed to the Gauda. Even if a school could not be built, something could be done about the school teacher. He was never in the village; he conducted school lying flat on his back in a cot. A complaint should be sent to the Inspector of schools. The Gauda was unwilling to complain: "The school teacher is a poor man, our policy should be to live and let live."

Sometimes, the Village-Level Worker comes to Gopalpur. It is his task to visit the five villages assigned to him and help the farmers to increase production. The Village-Level Worker lives seven miles from Gopalpur. Much of his time is occupied with the writing of progress reports describing the manner in which the villages under his charge have voluntarily cooperated to increase production dramatically, to introduce sanitary measures, and to build playgrounds and school houses. Some of the villages under his charge have done these things, but when the Village-Level Worker visits Gopalpur, he goes to the Gauda's house. The Gauda gives him a good meal. They discuss politics and philosophy during the heat of the day. In the evening, the Gauda gives the Village-Level Worker a cup of tea and sends him back. No one in Gopalpur needs a loan, no one will build a compost pit, no one will dig a drainage pit to keep mosquitoes from breeding in the village streets.

Everyone fears that the Gauda is the last of his kind in Gopalpur. Everyone knows that the government is going to replace Village Headmen and Village Accountants with elected officials and that it is going to take land away from large landholders and divide it among the poor. Even if this did not happen, the Gauda's property would be divided among his three sons, who would then be only slightly wealthier than other people in Gopalpur. Furthermore, it is evident that the Gauda's sons will leave the village to take up government employment. One son is already a school teacher in a distant town; another is taking professional training at the local college. Under the shadow of this predictable future, the Gauda practices a defensive, withholding strategy. He performs his traditional duties ineffectively, and blames his failures as an arbitrator of disputes upon the rebelliousness of the village. In the meantime he continues to demand that others meet their traditional obligations to him.

Danda and Chinta

On the other side of the village stands a row of houses belonging to the Farmer jati. The dwellings front upon a narrow street, so that the comings and goings of the members of any one household inevitably disturb the members of all the other households. In one of these houses lives Danda, an old man noted for his remarkable success in the practice of agriculture. Danda and his family follow a strategy of hard work and thrift. Danda explains:

People in this village say that the Gauda is a big man. In fact, he is nothing. The production from even one of my fields would fill this house. People are amazed when they see a person like myself leading his life without difficulty even though there are twenty-five people in the house. They cannot understand why I don't have to borrow from others. Sir, I will tell you a story.

A man lived in a certain place. He was not willing to work. When he couldn't get food he said, "God gave me birth and he is responsible for my food. He must feed me today." He sat and waited, without trying to find food anywhere. On seeing this, God felt tired and said to himself, "The poor fellow will die if I don't give him some bread." So God threw a piece of bread down in front of the man. The bread touched the man's hand and fell to the ground. The man tried to pick it up, but the bread sank into the ground. The man dug into the ground, but the bread continued to sink. The man became tired and said to himself, "Even though I do not want to work, God is a tricky fellow; he is making me work." The man began to dig in the ground; finally, he found the bread and ate it. After that he began to work hard.

Whatever the reason might be, Danda has had a successful life. The old man has six sons, all of whom are literate. All but the youngest is married. Years ago, the old man purchased lands four miles from the village in the bed of an abandoned irrigation tank. The lands were rich, but there was no easy way of getting manure from the village to the bed. Somehow, using two pairs of bullocks to pull a cart, Danda and his children managed to manure the field and to harvest, year after year, rich crops. When there is a fair, the heads of other families give their sons money to spend on refreshments. Danda's sons attend the fair carring a basket of mangoes. They sell them and purchase their refreshments from the proceeds.

In some respects, both Danda and the Gauda have followed the same strategy. Both have placed the interests of their own families ahead of the duties of the man of wealth. The accumulation of wealth by the Gauda is expected; it is part of the image of a Gauda. The accumulation of wealth by a Farmer is another matter, for it not only threatens the position of the Gauda, but that of every other farmer in Gopalpur. There is only so much land in Gopalpur; what one man farms cannot be farmed by another. Although Danda, by developing distant lands, has expanded the economy of Gopalpur, people do not think of his achievement in terms of the creation of wealth. They think rather that Danda's success contributes to their own failure.

Next door to Danda lives Chinta. Although Danda and Chinta were friendly for many years, this relationship was soured when Danda's fortunes increased and Chinta's declined. Every day, the members of Chinta's family watched the fat cattle and healthy children of the Danda family going back and forth on the street in front of their house. One day, four or five years ago, one of Danda's children drove his cattle home in the evening. After tying the cattle in the house, the young man went back into the street and began collecting the manure which his cattle had dropped. Chinta's younger brother was also collecting manure. The two young men, normally the best of friends, began to quarrel. They threw stones at each other and Danda's child was killed. Chinta's brother was arrested, but Chinta managed to have the charges dismissed, after his brother had spent three months in jail.

Chinta and his family were afraid that the Dandas would now avenge the death of their brother. Not long after Chinta's brother had been released from prison, Chinta, his brother, and one of his sons stood outside the Dandas' house, seeking to frighten them to the point where they would give up any thought of revenge. The Dandas were inside, with the door locked. The Chintas shouted insults and accused them of being cowards. Suddenly the door opened and the Dandas attacked with wood knives, killing Chinta's brother. Chinta and his son were seriously wounded and had to be taken to the hospital in Yadgiri.

For several months, Chinta and his son were afraid to return to Gopalpur, and lived with a sister in a nearby village. When they did return to Gopalpur, it was with the announced intention of killing Danda's oldest son. A friendly landlord in a neighboring village found jobs in a steel mill for Danda's oldest son and two of his younger brothers. The two youngest brothers, who had not been involved in the fighting, remained in Gopalpur.

In the meantime, Chinta's oldest son, never a fighter, became a storekeeper. Chinta filled the mind of his next oldest son with thoughts of revenge. Leaving him to work in the fields, Chinta devoted his time to village politics, showing his scars to whoever would listen to his threats against Danda's son. Chinta's most important ally was the Gauda, although it is not clear why he supported Chinta. Many people thought that he was afraid of Chinta; some thought that he wished to use Chinta to control persons in the village who were borrowing money from other landlords and rising to positions of economic power. The Gauda's support of Chinta consisted in not reporting the thefts and assaults committed by Chinta and his supporters. The Gauda's failure to take action to prevent further conflict between the two families could have been due to fear or to vacillation. Another factor might have been that every year the Gauda auctions land in the bottom of an irrigation reservoir for the growing of wheat. The parties led by Danda and Chinta bid against each other, each trying to outdo the other in promising profits to the Gauda.

Storekeeper and the Crier

Conflict in Gopalpur is not limited to that in the Farmer jati between Danda and Chinta. The Saltmaker jati and the Shepherd jati are also divided by conflict, and members of these two jatis belong to both the Danda and Chinta parties. Although there are many Saltmakers in Gopalpur, there are relatively few Saltmakers in other villages. For this reason, many marriages within the Saltmaker jati take place between the Crier's lineage and the Storekeeper's lineage. Not all of these marriages have been successful. The Crier's wife died several years ago, and he has since devoted himself entirely to the care of his eight-year-old son. He refuses to remarry because he fears that a stepmother might mistreat his boy. The Crier passes his days lying on his cot and caring for his son. On occasions when the son is not "sick" and in need of constant attention, the Crier is busy chatting with Chinta and discussing politics with members of Chinta's party. The Crier's younger brother carries on necessary labors in the family fields. The younger brother admires the Crier because the Crier is educated and important. Educated men, like the Gauda, are not supposed to work.

The Crier's sister is married to Storekeeper, who maintains a small shop on the other side of the village. Storekeeper and his wife are childless, but have adopted Storekeeper's brother's daughter. Two of Storekeeper's brothers have permanent employment in Bombay and Storekeeper visits them frequently, taking with him a five-gallon can of butter which he sells on the blackmarket. Afflicted with chronic stomach pain, fluttering nervously about his shop, Storekeeper is a successful small businessman. Storekeeper owns a horse which is bigger than that of the Gauda and his shop is more profitable than that run by Chinta's oldest son. Storekeeper is considerably less generous than Chinta's son.

Danda, Chinta, the Crier, and Storekeeper are major figures in the politics of Gopalpur. They take their place in politics by virtue of the active attempts they make to line up supporters and to extend their circle of influence. Each of these men has a circle of relatives and friends. A few of the Shepherds, and all of the Stoneworkers, maintain a precarious neutrality. To maintain their position of leadership and to appeal to those who are neutral, these four must establish the fact that, in any conflict, they are the injured parties. This is relatively easy for Chinta, because no one blames Chinta or his son if they are overcome by rage and make violent attacks on persons who stand in their way. Chinta's brother was killed by Danda's son. Chinta's ally, the Crier, has more difficulty in rationalizing his position, because he is a government official and should therefore be neutral. Further, neither Crier nor Storekeeper can afford to develop a permanent enmity, for they are "mother's brother" to each other, and each depends upon the other for brides and bridegrooms for his family and lineage. Although Danda and Chinta both belong to the same line, they are "brothers," both give their daughters to the same families. Thus, there are restraints upon the conflict between Danda and Chinta.

For these reasons, the "war" between the two parties in Gopalpur is a war of attrition. Chinta's party goes out into the fields to rehearse a drama without disturbing the village. They practice until three in the morning. When they return home at dawn, each carries a sack of grain from Danda's field. While the grain is being cut, Danda hides, thinking they may have come to kill him. A few nights later, a cow belonging to one of Chinta's supporters comes home limping. Someone has thrown a stone at it. Storekeeper's wife leaves her bed in the yard, where everyone sleeps during the warm nights. Instead of awakening her husband and going into the house with him, she goes into the fields and meets Chinta's son. A few days later, Chinta's wife meets a Shepherd, a friend of Storekeeper while she is gathering wood in the forest. A few days later, a sheep is boiling in Chinta's cooking pots, and his friends are eating mutton. An architect of bold and adventurous schemes, his life already in pawn for that of his brother, Chinta is a far more successful thief than his rivals. Although Chinta and the Crier lack sufficient wealth to invest in lavish entertainment, nevertheless they manage to attract and feed a large following. Cautious and legalistic, not enjoying the support of the Gauda, Danda and the Storekeeper are somewhat less successful in the war of attrition. They hope that, eventually, the excesses of the other party will swing popular support to their side.

Until such time as the balance of power swings definitively in one direction or another, the leaders of both parties are under a compulsion to demonstrate their opposition to conflict. This compulsion arises from the obligation to hold the village fair and to perform calendrical ceremonies essential to the welfare of the village, as well as to the preservation of Gopalpur's reputation within the region. For when Gopalpur ceases to perform ceremonies, it also neglects to return the concurrent hospitality of other villages. It is also important that Gopalpur send a wrestling team to the neighboring fairs where its enemy village seeks to defeat it. If all of the young men of Gopalpur do not go as a team to the wrestling matches, a humiliating defeat becomes inevitable. Chinta's son and Danda's son walk side by side to the fair and perform as members of the team, their sworn enmity forgotten for the occasion. Danta and Chinta, Storekeeper, and the Crier, attend all ceremonies, each radiating friendliness and goodwill.

Tamma

Gopalpur's leaders are generally thoughtful strategists. Their competition takes place in the borderline zone where the rules are unclear, and where they can appeal to their followers by presenting their own interpretations of right and wrong. The situation is different when a leadership role is forced upon a man who would otherwise be a minor character in the social drama. Such a man is Tamma.

In 1957, Tamma's older brother's wife died. To earn money for a second marriage, Tamma and his older brother went to work for the Gauda. Storekeeper, the leader of Tamma's lineage within the Saltmaker jati, advised Tamma to devote his attention to the support of his own family. A man's moral responsibility to his brother ends when the brother is married. Further, it is the older brother who arranges the marriage of the younger brother, not *vice versa.* With his older brother widowed and childless, Tamma would have inherited the family property and his many children would have been adequately provided for. Tamma refused to separate from his older brother and both brothers began working for the Gauda.

For various reasons, Tamma and the Gauda did not get along. In a village of hardworking and saturnine men, Tamma was remarkably talkative. It is a matter of record that Tamma was constitutionally unable to complete an errand requiring fifteen minutes in anything less than an hour. Instead of sleeping in the Gauda's garden with the other workmen, Tamma was too often found sleeping in his own house. Although Tamma was remarkably loyal, he was impertinent and ambitious. Tamma's oldest child was one of the five children enrolled in the village school.

When the Strangers came to Gopalpur, the Gauda decided to give Tamma to the Strangers. It was known that foreigners always underpaid their servants, that they made them work hard, and that they were fond of kicking and beating them for even the slightest error. The Gauda told Tamma that he was being sent to work for the Strangers because he was a person whom the Gauda could trust to report everything the Strangers did. To the Strangers the Gauda said, "Make him work hard, pay him no more than twenty rupees a month, keep him with you night and day." When the Gauda called on the Strangers, he inquired about Tamma, who was almost invariably eating or on the way to the neighboring village to collect the mail. These processes involved hours spent in relaying information concerning the Strangers to hundreds of eager ears. In time, the Gauda discovered that Tamma was being paid thirty rupees per month.

To make matters worse, a kind of greatness had been thrust on Tamma. He made weekly trips to Yadgiri to purchase foodstuffs for the Strangers, and many of the great men of Yadgiri made use of that wagging tongue to acquire secret knowledge of the Strangers' behavior. In full and exclusive charge of the intimate details of the Strangers' peculiar methods of preparing food, trained in the remarkable rituals accompanying the use of a kerosene stove and the scientific washing of dishes, Tamma found a willing, even admiring audience wherever he went: "In their country nobody does any work, all of the work is done by machines. They drink nothing but hot water. When it is night here, it is daytime in their country. Just to travel from their country to this country costs three thousand rupees. They are great people."

Tamma's rise from insignificance to greatness was observed with bitterness, not only by the Gauda, but by Tamma's relative, the Crier. Blind to his own younger brother's obvious faults, the Crier was determined that he should replace the lazy and ineffectual Tamma as the Strangers' servant. "Tamma," the Crier announced, "is a thief. When he goes to your house to work, he passes the open door of my house. Who knows what he might steal?" The next day, the Crier made a further point, "The house which you are renting belongs to my family. No one but members of my family should be allowed to work there." Not only the Crier, but many other people in the village, were amazed by the Strangers' knowledge concerning the price of the articles which they purchased in the village. In discussing rent for the house, the Crier had pointed out that in Bombay such a house would rent for one hundred rupees. The Strangers had refused to pay more than fifteen rupees. It was suspected that Tamma was secretly giving the Strangers information concerning the cost of things. In fact, the same moral principles that prevented Tamma from separating from his brother, prevented him from participating in plans to fleece the Strangers.

The Beginnings of Conflict

One of Tamma's friends was Kala, a farmer. Kala had at one time worked for the Gauda. Of recent years, Kala had discovered that there was always a way in which a clever man could earn his living. Noted for his singing and organizing ability, Kala was a guest at every party. His fertile brain conceived scheme after scheme designed to earn money without working. Many of these, directed at the Gauda and at the Strangers, were successful. Kala had little difficulty in extracting twenty-five rupees from Tamma in order to embark upon an unusually ambitious plan. Going to the Yadgiri market with Tamma, Kala brought back a five-gallon tin of cooking oil and a large supply of flour. He took as his working partner an industrious young Muslim, established a shop, and began manufacturing fried delicacies. Some of these were sold to the Strangers; the remainder were sold to watchmen in the village fields. In particular, Kala carried his basket of delicacies to fields that were being guarded by employed watchmen, rather than by members of the field owner's family. The purchasing currency was the ripening grain of the fields. Only too often, the watchmen enjoyed a feast at the Gauda's expense. After a few days, during the heat of noon when the streets were empty, Chinta's son broke into the room where Kala stored his oil and flour, and removed the supplies to his house.

Kala complained to the Gauda. The Gauda interrogated Kala and Tamma, "Who is the thief?" Kala and Tamma said nothing. The Gauda said, "You are protecting the thief, how can I report this matter to the police if you refuse to name the thief?" Tamma brought a witness. The Gauda considered, "If Chinta's son is the thief, you must search his house to see if the cooking oil is there." Only the week before, Chinta's son had argued with a Stoneworker and slashed his leg with a shovel. Kala and Tamma refused to search Chinta's house. The Gauda turned to the Strangers, "You see, these people all stick together. When I try to deal with crime in this village, they refuse to cooperate with me." To Kala, the Gauda said, "Now, you are without work. Why don't you work for me?"

The marriage of Tamma's older brother brought Tamma once more into the center of Gopalpur politics. After securing a loan from a landlord in a neighboring village, Tamma found a divorced woman with two children and arranged a marriage. The divorce had occurred under unusual circumstances. The husband had disappeared and was nowhere to be found. This was an advantage in that there was no need to return the bride price to the husband. Perhaps if Tamma had not been a younger brother, unskilled at the arrangement of marriages, he would have inquired more deeply into the circumstances that would lead a man to desert his wife and his investment. When Tamma invited Storekeeper to the wedding, Storekeeper refused to attend unless the Crier agreed to give up his friendship with Chinta. Storekeeper's wife was the Crier's sister. She, and the entire jati of Saltmakers, had been dishonored by Chinta's son. The Crier refused to abandon his friendship.

Thus, in arranging for his brother's marriage, Tamma encountered a series of value conflicts. The first of these concerned whether a man's first duty is to his older brother or to his own wife and children. Evidently Tamma's decision to place the interests of his older brother over those of his wife and children was an error, for it led to a second value conflict. Should Tamma delay his brother's marriage until Storekeeper and the Crier have settled their dispute, or should Tamma go ahead with the wedding? As a younger brother, Tamma lacked the stature and the political experience that would have enabled him to resolve this conflict successfully. Tamma held his brother's wedding.

The brother's new wife was beautiful, and Tamma's brother had fallen in love with her at first sight. Customarily, any children old enough to be weaned are left with the bride's parents when she remarries. The new wife refused to send her children away. Tamma's older brother did nothing. While Tamma's wife was lying in bed, greatly weakened by the delivery of her fourth child, the new wife fell upon her and beat her, and refused to serve meals to her. Later, she refused to serve Tamma or his children, announcing to her husband that it was foolish to continue to feed them since their share was half of the family property. The six members of Tamma's family should eat no more than the four members of her family. Tamma's older brother did nothing. When the new wife beat Tamma's mother, her husband told her to mend her ways. Finally, Tamma's brother sold the plow bullocks and left the village, leaving Tamma to work out his future as best he could.

While Tamma was suffering from the sharp tongue and hard heart of the woman he had chosen as his brother's wife, the Crier demanded vengeance. Tamma's failure to extend an invitation to the wedding was an insult not to be borne by an honorable man. "Tamma must die," the Crier pronounced. Of course, if Tamma wished to preserve his skin, he could give up his job with the Strangers, and the Strangers could then hire the Crier's younger brother. With the uncharitable Tamma out of the way, not only the Crier, but the Crier's friends as well, could count on a lavish distribution of food and gifts at the hands of the Strangers.

The Fight

So matters continued until the night of July fourteenth. For several weeks, a cold wind had blown across the rain-soaked fields of the village. A month ago, the sky was clear and the village fields were as hard as concrete and seamed with great cracks. Except for a few trees, everything was dead under a white sky filled with blinding light. Now, in the middle of July, the land is green, the sky is leaden gray, and the village streets are a sea of mud and cow dung. It is the time of Muharram, "Allah's festival." The Muslim shrine near the village gate has been vacated by the Silversmith and his family. During the day, the Muslim Priest and other Muslims have painted the shrine in broad stripes of red and white. Geometric silver standards, representing five different gods and saints, have been lined up against the wall of the godhouse. The base of each one has been dressed in elegant clothing; flowers and mango leaves decorate them and the godhouse. The pit in front has been cleaned out, and a fire burns brightly there. Beyond, there is an open space, where, a bonfire has been built. At ten o'clock in the evening, the village goes in procession, carrying brilliant kerosene pressure lanterns, making offerings at the village gate and at the various godhouses. The procession stops at the Muslim godhouse, the lanterns are hung from the walls, and the drummers take their places near the bonfire. Women and children crowd together on stone benches surrounding the godhouse and the open space in front of it. Men, carrying staffs and pieces of cloth in place of the spears and shields usual to the Muharram procession, take their place around the fire. They begin to dance in a circle while, led by the Singer, they sing *bhajane* songs, and mark time by striking their sticks on the ground. When they have warmed up, the drumming changes and they begin to dance facing away from the fire, stepping sideways around it. Every few steps, the men leap in the air, turn to face the fire, wave their staffs and shields in a threatening manner, and shout, "Bussayya."

Towards one o'clock, there is a pause in the dancing. Tamma and Storekeeper and one or two of their friends sit on a stone in the darkness far from the light of the pressure lantern. Suddenly there are yells and war cries. There is the sound of staffs being brought down on heads and shoulders. There are cries of anguish. Young men emerge into the light of the fire swinging eight-foot staffs with both hands, and jumping up and down like the warriors in the drama.

The Mavla, as Police Headman, rushes into the fray. He seizes the Stranger by the arm and drags him unwillingly into the center of the battle. The warriors disperse and the night becomes quiet. Only fifty or sixty older men and neutrals remain to dance around the fire. They dance slowly. One of them shouts an insult at another, and the dancing ceases. The Mavla, standing near the bonfire, begins to tremble and his legs shake. His mouth opens and there is a tortured, unearthly scream. He runs at people standing near the fire, who give way in terror. He dances toward the fire in front of the godhouse, then back. Again he dances toward the fire, and this time dances through it, his feet scattering the burning coals. In front of the godhouse, he speaks in the angry, threatening tones of the god of the Turks; "If the people quarrel, they will have dirt for food." Then he falls to the ground before the standards representing his deities.

In the morning, one of the standards, representing Kishan Sab, is carried to the tomb of Shah Hussein. Drums beat, and boys wearing cowbells dance around the standard. The man bearing Kishan Sab is possessed, and dances with a strange, jerking motion. Offerings of brown sugar and sandalwood are made to Shah Hussein. The procession then goes to the Hanumantha godhouse, where the two deities greet each other. The procession returns to the Muslim godhouse and the worshipers disperse.

Aftermath

In the afternoon, Saltmaker and Tamma and two or three of their friends gather at the Gauda's house to exhibit their bruises. The Gauda announces that he will settle the dispute as soon as Chinta and the Crier come. The Crier's nephew fills the Crier's role, going from place to place to search for the missing men. They are not to be found. In the late afternoon, Chinta comes. He says, he had nothing to do with the trouble, neither he nor the Crier were even present.

The next day, two policemen come to the village and sit on the veranda of the Gauda's house. They ask the Mavla and the Gauda why they had not submitted a report of the riot. They insult the Gauda and the Mavla. They interview the Crier, "How can you, a government official, participate in such an affair?" They send the Crier to purchase cigarettes and matches and the Mavla for tea and milk, but they do not pay for anything. They ask when the next bus will pass along the road two miles from the village. There will not be another bus, so they decide to spend the night here, and demand food and lodging. In the morning, they take the nine victims and assailants to headquarters. Victims and assailants pay their own bus fares and treat the staff of the police station to a hearty meal. In the evening, they return after signing elaborate documents promising never to quarrel again. Chinta and the Crier have to leave again immediately. One of the important men in the neighboring village of Yelher has sent for them. He tells them that members of their party will not receive loans of grain at the time of the fall sowing.

The village is quiet through the harvesting of the rainy season crop and the sowing of the fall crop. The first of November is *Dipavli*, the Festival of Lights. It is not an important festival in Gopalpur, but it marks the beginning of the fiscal New Year. The storekeepers decorate their stores and the priest comes to make appropriate inscriptions on their account books. All night long, both Chinta's son and Storekeeper entertain their clients.

The next night, at ten in the evening, Chinta appears before Danda's house accompanied by his second son. Danda's wife is standing outside on her veranda holding a lantern high, while her husband and sons are in the street in front of the doorway. A crowd has gathered, but keeps at a safe distance. Danda shouts angrily at Chinta, "Three times you have sent your son to my field to beat my son." Chinta denies the accusation, "My son was looking for cattle which had strayed." He dares Danda to send three men from his house to fight it out with three men from Chinta's house. Danda says, "Name the time and place, we'll be there. What about tomorrow morning?" Chinta says, "I am ready right now, come on." Danda refuses to fight in the dark. Chinta says, "You are nothing but women."

The Mavla and the Crier stand between Danda and Chinta. The Crier suggests that it would be pleasant if everyone lived in his own house and minded his own business. Gradually, the distance between Danda and Chinta increases. After two hours, Chinta reluctantly returns to his own house, and the crowd disperses. A few months before, the Crier had purchased brandy and used it to fire up the spirits of the young men who beat Tamma and the Storekeeper. This night the Crier acts the role of peacemaker.

The parties continue their activities. On November 14th, two of the young men who had attacked Tamma beat a shepherd, using the iron spike from a harrow. In the evening, Chinta's party stages a drama. Storekeeper and Danda meet with their friends a few nights later to discuss the presentation of a second drama. There is great enthusiasm. Tamma addresses Danda's oldest son, "Your little brother would make a splendid Krishna." Danda's son replies, "I doubt that, I don't think he can read well enough. Your friend, the Shepherd would make a far better Krishna." The drama teacher, when he comes from the neighboring village, is dubious about the project. Disorder in Gopalpur has become a scandal in the area. He does not want his play broken up by rioting but, eventually, agrees to direct the play. In the spring, Gopalpur plans to stage a more elaborate fair than usual in order to demonstrate the absence of conflict in the village.

In December, the Crier's adoption of the role of peacemaker is explained. Not only has the web of relationships between Gopalpur and neighboring villages been used to restrict the conflict in Gopalpur, but the web of relationships within Gopalpur has begun to tighten. Storekeeper's father's brother's son, his classificatory brother, is married to the Crier's daughter. Her first menstruation has occurred. The Crier must either forfeit all rights as father of his daughter or he must, on the eighth day of his daughter's puberty ceremony, feed Tamma, the Storekeeper, and the assembled guests. For seven days, the bride and groom, dressed in new clothing, sit outside their house in the evening. Women gather and sing instructive songs, "Keep silent in your husband's house, don't gossip when you go to get water." On the morning of the eighth day, the Crier enters Storekeeper's shop with gifts. The Saltmaker jati assembles. In a few minutes all are friendly. That evening, the guests gather. There is a procession from the Crier's house to the groom's house. As people sit in front of the groom's house waiting for food to be served, word arrives that Chinta will not attend the ceremony. The Accountant and one or two other "Big Men" go to Chinta's house. Finally, Chinta appears. People sit to eat. The host and his assistants move up and down the line shouting, "Call out if your plate is empty, there is plenty of food." Guests shout, "Chinta's plate is empty; Shepherd Hanumantha looks hungry." When the meal is over, the women begin to sing. Towards midnight, five girls dressed in red saris perform a ceremony in honor of the bride. Puffed rice is distributed and the guests go home.

For the next few months, there will be harmony in the village. In time, a family will quarrel and its members will separate, two farmers will quarrel over a field or a piece of cow dung, or a husband will quarrel with his wife. The delicate balance of parties and alliances will shift and conflict will reoccur.

Again, pressures from the outside and the internal needs of the village will restore a kind of order. During 1960, Tamma will be brought before the Guada's house and beaten again. Later, the Gauda's house will be robbed. Police will come to the village again, but they will be unable to find the culprit. People in Gopalpur have ceased to defend the Gauda whom they spoiled and fondled when he was a child in the streets of the village. But as the Gauda's power wanes others continue the struggle for prestige and security.

7

Navira: The New Wind

Past and Future

IN MYSORE STATE, the term *navira*, new air, is used to describe the changes that have taken place in modern times. The new wind blows strongest near the great cities of India. In such places as Gopalpur, the new wind is more like the first faint stirrings of cold air marking the beginning of the change from night to day. People toss restlessly on their wooden cots, the cock crows, and there are murmurs of discontent. The new wind has had more impact upon the Eskimo, the Hottentot, and the aborigines of Australia than it has here.

In Gopalpur, the basis of life is as it has always been. Men plow in the same way; they deal with their friends and neighbors in the same way; they have the same virtues and vices their grandfathers had. For centuries, foreign visitors have come to the Gopalpur region to visit the nearby cities and empires of Bijapur, Vijayanagar, Golconda, and Gulbarga. There have been Buddhist monks from China; there have been Greeks, Romans, Arabs, Russians, Portuguese, Italians, and Englishmen. Those visitors who left behind them written records were often shocked at what they saw. They were upset by the failure of people in the region to follow the true religion, and they were astonished by the complexity of social relationships. Few of the early visitors to South India mention poverty or underdevelopment. Most were impressed by the great wealth of the land and the great size of the cities. Frequently, they found their own cold or dry homelands poor and primitive in comparison to what they considered to be the fabulous wealth of South India.

In recent years, more and more travelers have come from foreign lands to visit South India. Tourists peer out at the Gopalpur region through the barred windows of first class compartments on the train from Bombay to Madras. The fat beggars of Yadgiri gather about the train to proclaim that they are on the verge of starvation. The visitor is appalled by noise and poverty. When he can stand it no more, he bangs down the metal shutters on the windows of the compartment and falls asleep. The great cities seem shabby and dirty. The fertile plain seems hot, arid, and unproductive. Most visitors conclude that something has happened to Gopalpur and to villages like Gopalpur. They conclude that the ancient wealth is gone, that the land has lost its fertility, that what was once a rich country is now, somehow, a poor country.

But it is not so much that Gopalpur has changed as that the outside world has changed. The wealth seen by the ancient explorers of South India, and the poverty seen by its modern visitors, was and is more in the eye of the beholder than in the nature of the land. The soil of Gopalpur seems to produce neither more nor less than in 1800, when British officials made their first appraisals of newly conquered territories of Mysore State. There is a strong possibility that people in Gopalpur today are wealthier than they have ever been, since taxes have never been so low. There have been one hundred sixty years without war and nearly one hundred years without famine. The whimsical rule of petty kings has been replaced by a stable, bureaucratic form of government. The new government is, by all accounts, more efficient and more concerned with public health, education, and social welfare than any government that preceded it. The population of the region has increased, but it is not clear whether this is a sign of wealth or of poverty.

Whether or not Gopalpur is, in fact, richer or poorer than it was a hundred years ago, the new wind has brought to its people the sudden realization that they are now second-class citizens of the world. Only a few years ago, people felt that they were part of a great civilization and that most of the other people in the world were dirty, uncouth, and barbaric. Now the coin is most bitterly reversed. City people who come to Gopalpur descend from their jeeps slowly and cautiously, as if the very soil were defiling; they seem to detect some noxious odor in the village. People in Gopalpur have always admitted themselves to be uncouth, but they have always been proud of their skill at doing their job. They have considered themselves to be not just farmers, but the best farmers in the world. Now, even their ability to farm is treated with contempt. The traditional culture of Gopalpur contained the answer to every problem. The fathers and forefathers of people in Gopalpur weathered flood, famine, pestilence, and war and built great cities on the fertile plain. As the new wind blows, feelings of pride and greatness are replaced by feelings of poverty and helplessness.

Hanumantha wonders what will happen in the future, "I don't know what will happen, God knows. Because this is the Age of Kali, there will be a lot of change. There will be more and more sin and the world will fill with evil." An old man says, "In my time, there were no match sticks, there were no airplanes, there were no automobiles, there were no railways. Now that all of these things have come, we are poor. In your time, throughout the world, great things are happening. The country is going ahead and will not fall behind in the future. In my time, if we wanted to go somewhere, we walked or rode horseback. Now there is the railway, the airplane, and the electric light. From this, the country will become even greater, it cannot fall back. Whatever other great things happen, you observe them. For me, this is enough." A woman says, "In the old days, there was plenty of food. Everyone was happy. There was

justice; the king listened and gave proper decisions. There was a state of ful-
fillment and contentment. There were no quarrels. Now, there is a great difference. There is lying and thievery. Justice is absent. Many creations of intelligence such as airplanes and radios have been built, but crop yields have de-
creased. In the future the world will change. We will be unable to find food
and there will be much fighting and knavery."

The Agents of Change

Old Yadgiri is a collection of large stone houses huddled beneath a
granite hill upon which stands the ruined fortress representing the greatness of
Yadgiri's past. The shops of Yadgiri are large and crammed with merchandise
of every description. There are factories too, a soap factory, several plants engaged in processing peanut oil for shipment to the United States, and a plant
that produces the local leaf-wrapped cigarette. Yadgiri has a small private college and a modern hospital run by missionaries. There is even a small suburb
designed in the manner of motion picture dream houses. With the exception of
the missionaries, the merchant and professional class in Yadgiri is mainly concerned with its own problems. The wealth of Yadgiri comes from farmers living
in villages like Gopalpur, yet the merchants see no particular value in sharing
their resources of knowledge and money with these farmers. Although people
in Yadgiri are aware, for example, of the value of smallpox vaccinations, no
effort is made to vaccinate the rural population, or even to inform them that
free vaccinations are available and effective. Attempts at health education on
the part of the missionaries and the hospital staff are given no encouragement.
The basic attitude of the Yadgiri merchant can be summed up in the notion
that, there being only so much wealth, aid other than conscience-salving charity
will only make someone else wealthy at one's own expense. Even the progressive merchants, who desire the development and industrialization of the region,
seem content to leave matters in the hands of the already overburdened government.

Like the missionaries, the government officials in Yadgiri are set apart.
They live and work in isolated buildings that line the concrete road connecting
Old Yadgiri to the railway station. The men in the government buildings are
bureaucrats, permanently employed by the government, and transferred repeat-
edly, either as a punishment for bad performance or as a reward for good. Their
future is secure, but their movement upward within the hierarchy of officialdom
depends partly upon their education and partly upon their ability to keep their
service records free of black marks. They carry out programs developed in the
state and federal capitals, Bangalore and Delhi, and possess neither the freedom nor the inclination to develop programs for planned change relevant to
the Gopalpur region. The programs are developed by people who have never
seen Yadgiri and scarcely know that it exists. When the program cannot be
put into effect in Gopalpur or in the surrounding region, the local government
official bravely fills out records showing that the program has been imple-

mented. He shrugs his shoulders and says, "The worst they can do is transfer me and there can't be any place worse than Yadgiri."

The government officials attempt to introduce new crops, build schools and playgrounds, give agricultural advice, provide loans, construct housing for the underprivileged, dig wells, and conduct public health programs. The programs are not much different from those of any other nation. Some of them are effective, some ineffective. Sometimes there is graft and corruption; sometimes things are done with great efficiency. Some of the programs are ill-conceived and irrelevant to the needs of the Gopalpur region. The local government officials do the best they can. They contend against apathy, or what they consider to be apathy, on the part of the conservative business and professional men of Yadgiri. The younger government officials contend against the older; the honest against the corrupt. Many are cynical and angry, "One of the richest men in Yadgiri lets his children use the street for a latrine. The police dare not do anything. There is only one way to handle such people. What this country needs is a strong dictator who will shoot them."

Many officials and educated men in Yadgiri see no hope of change, while those who do not want it fear that far too much has already taken place. In fact, change in the Gopalpur region has become inevitable. While Yadgiri's merchants and officials debate among themselves the desirability of change, it presses in from every side. The basic question is whether Gopalpur's transition from the old order to the new is to be peaceful and orderly or bloody and disorderly.

Economic Change

Because the basic methods of food production in Gopalpur have not changed in hundreds, perhaps thousands, of years, the degree of potential improvement in its economy is enormous. Since the water table is nowhere below fifteen or twenty feet, irrigation wells could be dug to increase the yield tenfold. Many kinds of tropical and subtropical fruit trees will grow here, given the proper care and protected from goats. Introduction of new varieties of millet could double or triple production. Insecticides, adequate grain storage facilities, chemical fertilizers, rat poison, decent fences—these are some of the many things that could vastly increase productivity in a short time.

The farmer of Gopalpur conducts his agricultural operations on a scale which only a very wealthy country could afford. Rather than use proper amounts of seed of good quality and known germinating ability, the farmer scatters vast, wasteful quantities of unselected, untested seed. Failing to protect the young plants in the field, he perforce, shares his seedlings with every bird, insect, and wild animal that comes around. He heaps his manure and compost carelessly outside his door, unprotected from sun and rain. Instead of carefully storing his harvested crop, he places it in his house in clay jars or, worse on a crudely made stone floor. What the rats don't eat is drilled and powdered by worms and weevils.

There are reasons why the farmer in Gopalpur has not found a better way of doing things. A few men have tried to use chemical fertilizers. One year, the Village-Level Worker, a high school graduate from the city who has the task of instructing Gopalpur's farmers in the techniques of modern agriculture, urged five farmers to try the new fertilizer. They purchased some of the salty-looking stuff and, to guarantee success applied it liberally, even more liberally than the Village-Level Worker had advised. Before the next rain came, and it came slowly, the growing crop had withered and died. The next year, the same men, still friendly toward the Village-Level Worker, planted wheat in the bed of an empty irrigation reservoir. When the crop began to suffer from rust, the men obtained sulfur dust and a duster from the Village-Level Worker. They mixed the sulfur with buttermilk and attempted to spray the mixture with the duster. The duster, a fine machine which the government had imported from Germany, was ruined, and so was the crop. The hands of the Village-Level Worker are smooth and soft. His days are spent writing progress reports and keeping his office in order against the day when one of his superiors will pay a surprise visit.

Men in Gopalpur obtain seed for planting from Gaudas and wealthy men. At harvest time, they return two sacks of grain for every sack borrowed. When there is a wedding or a need for cash to buy bullocks, they borrow money from the same wealthy man. The wealthy man helps them when they encounter economic difficulties or when their security is threatened by their enemies. They dare not borrow from any other source. The wealthy man has little incentive to spend money on improved seed. He stands to gain little from improvements in his client's economic position; if the new seed fails, he will be blamed. There is no local agricultural experiment station, so there is no way of knowing whether new crops and agricultural techniques, developed in Bombay or Sussex or North Carolina, will be successful in Gopalpur.

At every step, the farmer wishing to improve his agricultural practices must weigh the claims of the new method against the known economic and social benefits of the traditional method. To purchase improved agricultural equipment, the farmer must sever his traditional relationship with the Blacksmith and Carpenter. This is more than an economic relationship. Not only are the Carpenter and Blacksmith neighbors and friends, but they have religious functions that make their presence essential on such occasions as birth, marriage, and death. The carpenter and Blacksmith offer an integrated set of tools and guarantee repairs. Under these circumstances, the purchase of a moldboard plow, or of any improved equipment, becomes a tricky and difficult business. On their side, the Carpenter and Blacksmith receive a fixed quantity of grain at harvest time. If they were to improve their product, they would find it difficult to raise their prices to cover its greater cost. The benefits of improved agricultural techniques have not been demonstrated, and their use is attended by great economic and social risk. In refusing to adopt new methods, the farmer of Gopalpur shows common sense, not conservatism.

Agriculture in Gopalpur is not a profitable industry. The farmer produces food in order to feed his family; he regularly sells only a small part of what he produces. If he paid wages to his family members, or paid cash for the fodder consumed by his animals, he would lose money every year. The farmer obtains money only when he sells his surplus production at harvest time. If he makes a profit from such sale, he uses the cash to pay off his debts, to send his children to school, to buy clothing, and to buy land, fertilizer, and agricultural equipment. Any change that requires money, whether it be the use of soap for bathing, the education of children, or the building of ratproof storage bins, depends upon the farmer's ability to sell his grain at harvest time for a profit that represents a reasonable reward for the time and money he and his family members have lavished upon his fields.

In most years, the price received by the farmer for grain is far below its true value, in terms of labor costs and capital investment. There are two reasons for this, the "harvest glut," and price control. Harvests occur at roughly the same time all over India, and because most farmers have poor grain storage facilities and a pressing need for cash, they must sell their grain promptly. The market tends to be glutted, with prices correspondingly low. The government controls the price of grain in two ways: through the introduction of rationing in the cities, and through the importation of foreign grain which it dumps on the market. The need to prevent price rises stems from the fact that city laborers and low-paid government workers spend most of their income on food and would starve if prices increased. The effect of price control is that the farmer, already the poorest man in India, is compelled to support not only the urban poor, but the wealthy and middle classes as well.

Changes in the methods of food production in Gopalpur, perhaps all change in Gopalpur, await the day that the farmer can make a profit from the sale of grain.

Those who make adequate profits and have acquired surplus capital are the large landholders in the Gopalpur region. They have been able to make changes in techniques of production because they have acreages large enough to yield a profit even when prices are low. The wealthiest man in one neighboring village uses chemical manure; the wealthiest man in another has purchased an American-made moldboard plow, so big that it must be pulled by three pairs of bullocks. Others have purchased jeeps and tractors. In Yadgiri, where there is access to seed catalogs and agricultural advice, new crops and new techniques are continually being introduced. The kinds of agricultural improvements introduced by those who farm large acreages are those which produce a reasonable yield with the least possible effort. These techniques are not applicable to the small farm in Gopalpur, because the small farm becomes an economically feasible operation only when the greatest possible yield is produced even though this demands the most possible effort. The large-scale farmer tends to cultivate "easy" grain crops, while the small farmer tends toward "hard" vegetable and orchard crops.

The changes that are being made in Gopalpur's production techniques favor relatively low-yielding crops that require large acreages and little labor. An iron moldboard plow calls for only half as much labor as does a wooden plow. Chemical fertilizers can be applied with considerably less labor than can cow dung and compost. Adequate manure, good seed, and healthy plants reduce the amount of labor needed for weeding, thinning, knocking insects off plants, and even for harvesting. Since, hitherto, the laborers of Gopalpur have found just enough work to permit health and survival, it is possible to conclude that even these slight changes in the farmer's use of hired labor would create massive unemployment. Twenty men, some with their families have already left Gopalpur to take up residence in a single, crowded apartment in a Bombay tenement. Some villages in the region have lost nearly half of their population to the booming industries of the big city. Many men in the Gopalpur region have already become "remittance men," living off small sums of money sent by relatives in the city.

People in Gopalpur rarely seek medical care at the hospital in Yadgiri, or even at the dispensary in the nearby village of Yelher. A man is considered to be sick only when he is incapable of working. For centuries, a high infant mortality, resulting from too frequent births and from endemic and epidemic diseases, has been a factor limiting the growth of population. Small pox, malaria, cholera, leprosy, dysentery, pneumonia, and the chronic worm diseases have been rampant. In recent years, the systematic programs of disease control, carried out locally and in other parts of India, have begun to have an impact. Inevitably, the life expectancy of children born in Gopalpur will increase. As people become healthier and live longer, there will be more people. Even if birth control were introduced, there is still a likelihood that it would permit a population increase, for births would be spaced, and healthier children and mothers would have a better chance for survival. At present, parents in Gopalpur who produce more children than they can support at the level of living to which they feel themselves to be entitled, deny medical care, and sometimes food, to their younger, weaker, or less attractive children. There is effective population control at present but, as people become more healthy and food becomes more readily available, the population will increase. In the relatively immediate future, a choice will have to be made between an ever-increasing population and an ever-increasing standard of living. At present, the people of Gopalpur seem to agree with most of the rest of the world's population that it is possible to have both.

Other Changes

Economic change has already begun to make itself felt in the Gopalpur region, if not in Gopalpur. But there are also a number of changes in village religion and social organization that the government officials, not to mention the missionaries, would like to make. To many government officials, a change in the moral character of the people of Gopalpur seems more fundamental and more important than any improvement in their economic condition. Government officials, and educated people generally, appear to be opposed to such practices as human sacrifice, animal sacrifice, institutionalized prostitution, arranged marriages, gambling, meat eating, drinking, concubinage, divorce, quarreling, landlords, inequalities among jatis, and time "wasted" on rituals and ceremonies. Although opposition to such practices as human sacrifice seems to stem from a newly developing international morality, the reasons behind some of the proposed changes are not clear. Meat eating, animal sacrifice, and ceremonies are things that go together in Gopalpur. Without them, people would have little animal protein in their diet, and the patterns of cooperation and competition that make possible the economic life of the village would be destroyed. Although Gopalpur generally believes itself to be more moral than the government officials, and the government officials believe themselves to be more moral than the people of Gopalpur, the problem is not basically one of moral superiority or inferiority, but of finding substitutes for those traditional practices that are now being condemned as immoral. People in Gopalpur do not know what to do *instead* of meat eating, animal sacrifice and ceremonies, nor do they know of any advantages to be gained by renouncing them. Government officials tell the people of Gopalpur that they are lazy and sinful, but they offer no positive remedies. The result is hostility toward government officials and spirited defense of the condemned traditional customs.

Government officials have been somewhat more successful in their attempts to reconstruct the social system of Gopalpur. The position of the Gaudas has been attacked by developing new sources of credit to give financial assistance to farmers and laborers. The democratic election of village officials, and the division of large land holdings, long threats, are soon to become law. These measures, which are designed in the long run to eliminate the class of landlords, fall short of replacing them. Landlords are the educated men of their villages, the innnovators who introduce new agricultural techniques, the protectors who alone are capable of dealing with police officials and settling conflicts. The credit extended by a landlord to a small farmer is a personal kind of credit. There is no due date for the loan, and the act of borrowing purchases the active support of the landlord when a family is attacked by other families within the village. Not all landlords fulfill their traditional roles adequately, but even when they do not, they remain the kingpins of the social structure of the villages they control. Many villages have irrigation reservoirs, wells, schools, and other improvements because their landlords were able to influence government officials. Although people in Gopalpur would be delighted at an opportunity to divide their Gauda's property among themselves, the prospect of there being no Gauda whatsoever fills most people with dismay.

The desire of government officials to raise the status of jatis which have been condemned to follow the more menial and less remunerative occupations occasions even more doubts. A farmer cannot weed and harvest his crop without labor. If those who now serve as laborers are converted into farmers, there will be no one to do the weeding and harvesting. Already, the missionaries have converted large numbers of people in the Gopalpur region belonging to the lower-ranking jatis. The new converts refuse to play drums at ceremonies, or to remove dead animals from the village streets. When Big Mother's water buffalo died, it lay rotting in its stall until well past midday, because the Leatherworkers refused to remove the carcass. Finally, during the afternoon, a committee of neighbors tied the animal's legs together, thrust a pole through them, and and angrily carried the animal to the outskirts of the village. Afterwards, the Leatherworker came and removed the skin. He denied Big Mother the traditional payment of a pair of sandals on the grounds that the skin was in bad condition. In almost every society but that of Gopalpur and similarly afflicted villages, there are persons who are clearly assigned such responsibilities as the removal of dead animals. People in Gopalpur are told that they must stop discriminating against people in low-ranking jatis, but they are not told what to do in order to obtain the services formerly performed by them.

The new wind blows in Gopalpur, however fitfully, and its effects are sometimes surprising. The government officials, charged with bringing the new wind to Gopalpur, work honestly and efficiently, insofar as it is possible for them to do so. At the same time, many changes which could be made are not being made. Government officials tend to lay the blame for lack of progress upon the people of such villages as Gopalpur, who in turn tend to lay the blame upon the government officials. Both groups feel helpless and apathetic. The new wind blows in an unchanneled and undisciplined way, stirring up new problems for every one solved. The source of the difficulty seems to lie in the government officials' failure to perceive the interrelationships among the things they are trying to change. The culture of Gopalpur is an organic whole; its religion and its social organization are adapted to the economic tasks traditionally carried out in the village. The reform programs stimulated by the new wind are not organic wholes. The new wind offers some hopeful and some frightening prospects, but it does not offer a way of life.

8

Gopalpur and Other Villages

Gopalpur within Its Region

A VILLAGE IS always a part of something larger. In the first chapter, Gopalpur was described in terms of its relationships to a material environment, but there is yet another kind of shape to a village, a shape that is molded by the interaction between the material environment on the one hand, and the regional and national culture, of which the village is but a fragment, on the other. A comparison between Gopalpur and other villages of the region serves to place it in proper perspective as one among many, for they are all merely islands in the same sea of communications and interactions. The shape of Gopalpur, therefore, derives in part from this sea of the regional culture. The very existence of the village is due to the fact that it is an element, in an agricultural civilization which has established villages throughout the region.

Some parts of the region are totally unsuited to agriculture, while some parts are suited to only one kind. The protection and control of both cattle and population require nucleated villages, in which farmers live together in a cluster of houses rather than on their own fields. Because some villages are established on fertile soil and some on infertile soil, not all can be the same size. Not all can support a complete staff of specialists and technicians to produce necessities or things considered to be necessities. Not all can produce the complete range of food stuffs needed to provide an adequate or satisfying diet. From this it follows that there must be an exchange of goods and services between them, and that the different villages concentrate on the production of specialized goods and services.

Gopalpur is a small village established on land of roughly average quality, producing salt, wool, and a wide range of food stuffs. It does not produce cigarettes, betel leaf, brooms, coconuts, bananas, cooking oil, cloth, blankets, or leather goods. These, and many other items, are purchased from neighboring villages with access to more favorable agricultural environments, or a larger population. In terms of economic function and size, it is possible to define four major types of villages, those settlements whose members are largely devoted to the practice of agriculture and related industries. The first kind of village is a hamlet that produces and exports only a few kinds of goods and services, and must import most goods and services used. The second kind is the "small village," like Gopalpur, that produces and exports many kinds of goods and services, but is dependent upon imports for a sizeable proportion of its daily needs. A "medium village" approaches self-sufficiency; relatively little of its economic life is taken up with the exchange of goods and services with other villages. A "large" or "market village" supports a sufficient number of specialists and specialized occupations to enable it to serve not only its own needs but those of surrounding villages as well. Within the region, these four kinds of villages form weakly defined circles of linked and "friendly" villages that are economically interdependent. Each of the villages within a circle performs different economic functions and, as a result, the pattern of living, the habits of work, the methods of child training, and the gradations of wealth and poverty, are different in each of them.

The social organizations of these related villages differ due to variations in size, to variations in the number, as well as the kinds, of jatis present, and to variations in the wealth and poverty of individuals within the community. Hamlets usually contain under three hundred people. The fields surrounding a hamlet tend to be rocky and unproductive. No one is wealthy, everyone is poor. Very often, hamlets contain representatives of only one jati, most frequently the Lambadies, who specialize in the transportation of firewood from distant forests to the larger villages. A few hamlets, possessing relatively rich soil, are occupied by members of the Farmer jati. Hamlets are not often visited by government officials. Fighting, theft, and other kinds of conflict rarely occur, and there are few ceremonies, no dramas, and no fairs. Almost nothing that is exciting or interesting ever happens. For entertainment, for jobs, and for almost all necessities, people living in hamlets must go to the larger villages.

Small villages, ranging in population from three to seven hundred people, offer greater variability than any other kind. Some are squeezed into peculiar ecological niches—small valleys in the hills where a temperate climate permits the production of betel leaf and areca nut; some are buffers filling in the gaps between larger villages; some occupy the transition zone between fertile lands that support large villages and desert lands that support hamlets or nothing at all. Depending upon the peculiar occupations or industries distinguishing it, the small village has its unique selection of jatis. Near the hills, where sheep may run freely, the small village may be dominated by the Shepherd jati. In the plains, it is more likely to be dominated by the Farmer jati or by the Lingayat Farmers. The presence of salt, farm land, and pasture land appears to have led to the development of three major jatis in Gopalpur—Farmers, Saltmakers, and Shepherds. Some small villages, with poor soil, or only one crop are likely to be dominated by the lowest-ranking jatis, and to export laborers at certain times of the year. Weakly supervised, rarely visited by government officials, small villages tend either to be autocracies ruled by a single strong man, or to be dominated by conflicts between middle-class farmers. Where small villages are dominated by Shepherds or Farmers or Lingayat Farmers, most are middle-class, and feature parties, violent conflicts, fairs, entertainments, and elaborate ceremonials.

Villages of medium size, containing between seven and twelve hundred people, are comparatively peaceful. They tend to occupy flat and favorable lands. They are composed of landlords, middle-class farmers, and laborers. A large number of different jatis are represented, and there is usually no single large dominant jati. Usually medium villages are unable to support any number of large landlords. The landlords are close relatives drawn from a minority jati, such as the Brahmins or the Reddi Landlords. Police and government officials visit frequently and the landlords tend to be progressive. The medium village has a good school and receives a fair amount of government assistance. Conflict occurs relatively rarely, but there are a number of fairs, dramas, and ceremonies.

The large village generally has a central location. Extensive irrigation, or particularly good soil gives it an edge over other villages. A very large spectrum of jatis is represented, and almost every kind of activity characteristic of the region is to be found. There are a number of large landlords, belonging to different jatis, who are likely to be in conflict with each other. Conflict in these villages derives its character from the political and economic conflict of the large landlords. Large villages contain the equivalent of a junior high school. Minor government officials, such as Village-Level Workers, are generally stationed there. The Headmen and Accountants of neighboring villages are often located in the large villages, which, in many instances, include a number of hamlets and small villages, for administrative purposes. Towns, such as Yadgiri, exceed large villages in size, but a large village may have up to six or seven thousand people, and contain thirty or more different jatis.

Neighboring Villages

Less than two miles south of Gopalpur is the Yelher Tanda, a hamlet composed of twenty Lambadi and five Farmer families. It is a collection of thatched houses, each having only one room. The Lambadi men dress like any other men in the region. The Lambadi women wear a bodice, a shawl of hand-printed material, and a skirt which is a patchwork of brightly colored pieces of cloth with bits of tin or glass sewn on. On her arms, the Lambadi woman wears bracelets of bone up to her elbow. As do the members of several other jatis, Lambadies speak their own language. The Lambadies are divided into clans, each with its own god or goddess. Members of each clan have representations of their clan god or goddess within their houses, but there are no god-houses in the village. The clans are grouped into exogamous moieties, so that a man cannot marry within his own clan or within the group of fraternally related clans. Three or four years before a marriage is to take place, an engagement is arranged between a man and a woman. The man then works for a landlord for four or five years, until he has accumulated enough money to pay the bride price of 600 rupees or four bullocks. If the wife dies and leaves a younger sister, the younger sister must be given to the widower. If a man's younger brother dies, he takes his younger brother's widow as his second wife. The chieftain of the hamlet is the *Nayak,* who inherits his position from his father, subject to the approval of the community. The Nayak officiates at the marriage ceremony.

The lands of the Yelher Tanda are a rocky wasteland on the side of a hill. Most of the families own less than eight acres apiece; thirteen of the twenty Lambadi families own four acres of land each. The land is poor; its major crops are peanuts and other hardy legumes. Almost all of the population work as laborers in nearby villages for a good part of the year. They also spend a good deal of time bringing firewood to the larger villages and selling it. There is no school in the Tanda and no one can read or write.

Less than a mile north of Gopalpur stands the village of Gannapur. Containing nearly two hundred households, Gannapur is larger and wealthier than Gopalpur. The dominant jatis in Gannapur are Lingayat Farmers, Farmers, and Shepherds. An important section of its population is vegetarian, which means that animal sacrifice is not a feature of village-wide ceremonials. The Gannapur Fair is celebrated in the name of the vegetarian deity, Hanumantha, in order to permit all of the members of the community to participate. The larger size of Gannapur entails a greater structuring of social relationships than in Gopalpur. The boundaries separating the different jatis tend to be more sharply drawn, and jatis tend to live together in their own sections of the village. In Gopalpur, friendships are frequently developed between people belonging to different jatis; in Gannapur, friends tend to come from the same jatis.

Gannapur's landlord left several years ago; the village now has no men of power or influence. As a result, even through Gannapur is relatively close to the main road, government officials visit rarely and perform few services for the village. Conflict, when it occurs, usually does so along jati lines, the Lingayat Farmers quarreling with the Farmers. Other jatis form alliances with one side or the other. Gannapur possesses no irrigated land. While Gopalpur has three definite agricultural seasons, Gannapur has only two.

East of Gannapur and Gopalpur stands the large village of Yelher. Yelher contains 672 households and nearly twice as many jatis as either Gannapur or Gopalpur. Nearly all the lands of Yelher consist of heavy black soil, suitable for the production of two crops per year, and much of it irrigated. Yelher is the wealthiest village in the region. The streets are lined with large houses, several of two stories. Many men are wealthier than Gopalpur's Gauda. There is a post office, a grammar school, a junior high school, a girl's school, and a cooperative society. The major jatis in Yelher are Reddi landlords and Farmers. About one sixth of the population formerly belonged to the lower-ranking jatis. Men from these jatis have been converted to Christianity, and there is a Christian school and dispensary. Where other villages boast only a handful of literates, more than 35 percent of the population of Yelher can read and write. Reddi landlords are active in state and local politics; government officials visit Yelher frequently, and landlords exert political pressure in attempts to obtain contracts for the building of roads, schools, and irrigation reservoirs. In Gopalpur, government officials are considered to be men of great power and influence; in Yelher, they are regarded as men to be influenced by bribes and threats. Political conflict in Yelher is always conflict among the great landlords, and often finds expression in the law court rather than in the street riot.

Seven miles north of Gopalpur, five hundred feet above the plains, stands the village of Chintanhalli. Just behind the village is a dam which provides irrigation water throughout the year. Chintanhalli contains 272 households of which nearly half belong to the Farmer Jati; the remainder belong to twenty-three other jatis. The unique aspect of Chintanhalli is its environment. Surrounding the village are acres of irrigated land where rice is grown. Surrounding the rice land are gardens devoted to the production of betel leaf, areca nut, fruit trees, and vegetables. The garden crops require continuous, intensive labor. Unlike most other villages in the region, Chintanhalli contains very few persons of average wealth. The population is divided between land owners, who are generally wealthy, and laborers, who are generally landless. A fair number of the wealthier landowners of the village have moved to a neighboring village that is closer to the road and offers more amenities. Motor vehicles cannot reach Chintanhalli and, as a result, government development programs have had little impact upon the village. There is no organized conflict in Chintanhalli, but there have been three murders in five years. The landless laborers of Chintanhalli express themselves through theft, murder, and flight. Over 180 persons have migrated to Bombay and other large cities. The landlords defend their position through beatings and arrests. Such conflict between landlords and laborers is to be found in very few villages in the region. It appears to derive ultimately from the fact that land in Chintanhalli is too expensive to be purchased by small or middleclass farmers and demands intensive labor. As a result, there is a marked contrast between rich and poor.

East of Chintanhalli is the village of Tatalgiri. Located on the dry slopes of the hills, Tatalgiri has almost no irrigated land and very little fertile land suitable for the fall planting. Essentially, Tatalgiri has only one crop season. It contains slightly over one hundred households, two thirds of them belonging to the Shepherd jati. There are two relatively wealthy families; the remainder of the population consists of landowning small farmers who, unlike the small farmers of the plains villages, do not produce enough to support themselves throughout the year. Few people in Tatalgiri are in debt: the loans could never be repaid. Most of the families plant and harvest their crops during the rainy season; they then leave the village during the fall to serve as laborers in other villages. During the hot season, people return to cut firewood in the nearby forest. Conflict in Tatalgiri takes place within the Shepherd jati which is divided into two parties.

The villages surrounding Gopalpur resemble Gopalpur in many ways. There are the same kinds of houses; people dress in the same ways, many of the same jatis are present. At the same time, each village represents a unique compromise between environmental circumstances and the regional patterns of culture. The patterns of labor, of social interaction, and of religious action differ in the various villages. Some villages, like Yelher can be defined as progressive. Some, like Gopalpur and Tatalgiri, as conservative. In the smaller villages, boundaries between different jatis tend to weaken while, in the larger, lines are drawn more sharply. The sharing of common poverty or common middle-class status leads to the creation of a democratic, egalitarian social organization in such villages as the Yelher Tanda and Gannapur. Gross differences in economic status lead to the emergence of marked social classes and an authoritarian social organization such as that of Chintanhalli.

Elephant

The people in most of the villages of the Gopalpur region speak Kannada, the official language of Mysore State. Politically, the Gopalpur region is a part of Mysore State. A comparison of the Gopalpur region with other regions in the state might begin with consideration of the village of Elephant, 360 miles south of Gopalpur, near the banks of the Cauvery River. Elephant, like the villages of the Gopalpur region, is located far away from the nearest city. Where the Gopalpur region consists largely of plains, the region around Elephant is made up largely of hills broken by small valleys. Where the Gopalpur region contains hundreds of villages, Elephant is one of twenty-one villages in its region. People living in Elephant marry within their own region which contains between ten and fifteen jatis. Most of the people of the Elephant region belong to the Lingayat jati.

Elephant's poet, a man feared throughout the Elephant kingdom for his sharp tongue, introduces his village as follows:

> The town stands
> Where two streams join.
> There are sixteen shops
> And big business is going on.
>
> Fruits and vegetables
> Come on the bus tops.
> A coconut worth an anna
> Sells for six or more.

Villagers, quarreling among themselves,
Crowd the market.
They carry headloads
And quarrel among themselves.

Leaving the town,
They reach the stream near the hamlet.
If they look straight up,
They can see Elephant.

Climbing stone stairs,
Climbing stone stairs again,
They come to a boundary marker.
Across the boundary stands Elephant.

There are fifty-five families here,
All strong worshippers of Siva.
Singing plowing songs, they grow millet.
They live in pride, fearing none.

The long gauda, the short village menial.
The deaf chieftain, these three men
Joined in conspiracy with five others
And our taxes were greatly increased.

The life of the happy children was wrecked
When some village elders,
Hearing some screams, came running.
For sixty dirty rupees, they granted a divorce.

If there is a commotion and a call
To drive wild elephants and boars from the fields,
The elders run wild on the stony paths
And drive the animals away from their fields.
If there is a call to worship at the temple,
They sleep by the side of their wives.

Elephant is situated approximately two thousand feet above sea level, and is colder all year than Gopalpur. From the termination of the bus line to the village of Elephant is approximately two miles, the second mile of which consists of a stone staircase, rising five hundred feet from the floor of the plain to the top of the hill upon which Elephant is located. Surrounding Elephant are terraced fields cut into the side of the hill. The fields are covered with fruit trees, and the forest presses close on every side. Although it is only two miles from Elephant to the foreign village situated at the end of the bus line, it is seven miles from Elephant to the nearest neighboring village within Elephant's region. A small, recently established hamlet is somewhat closer.

Houses in Elephant are the size of the smallest houses of the Gopalpur region. Uniformly, they contain a small cooking place and just enough space so that the family members, lying side-by-side, have enough room to unroll their bedding and sleep. In Elephant, people sleep on the floor inside the house; it is too cold to sleep outside. When the house is overcrowded, a few of the menfolk move to the village godhouse and sleep there. The houses have walls of pressed mud made in successive layers about eighteen inches high. The roof consists of a framework of bamboo covered with thatch or tile. The floor is plastered with cow dung. In the daytime, bedding is rolled up and stored on a bamboo platform underneath the rafters.

Women in Elephant dress in much the same way as women in Gopalpur. Men wear short trousers, a shirt, often sleeveless, and a towel. One or two slightly wealthier men wear the long dhoti of Gopalpur; a few men wear shorter wrap-around dhoties. Men who can afford neither a dhoti nor a pair of short trousers wear a strip of cloth six inches wide, passed between the legs and supported by the waist cord which everyone wears. In Gopalpur, new clothing is distributed four times a year; in Elephant, family heads purchase clothing twice a year. Everyone in Elephant, except the two families of Leatherworkers, wears a silver box around his neck, symbolizing membership in the Lingayat jati.

Dominating all other buildings in Elephant are the godhouse and the "monastery," and dominating all other men is the Priest. The godhouse is open on one side, and holds the sacred images of Basava, Šiva, and other Lingayat deities. The front part is a public rest house, where travelers sleep and are entertained. Beside it stands the monastery, which is a rectangular structure of many rooms built around an open courtyard. Ultimately, the monastery will house the Priest and will serve as a resthouse for pilgrims and other visitors to Elephant. It has not yet been completed.

Except for the Leatherworkers, the people of Elephant are vegetarians. There are no sheep or goats or chickens in the village. The diet consists of cow's milk and hard-cooked red millet mush, formed into balls. The balls of red millet are dipped into a soup made from eggplant, chilies and other vegetables. Each family eats privately inside its own house, to which no one else but the Priest and close relatives is admitted. The people consider themselves to be among the last upholders of jati purity in an impure world. Elephant is a theocracy ruled absolutely by its Priest and a few leading men. Although these rulers sometimes indulge in heated discussions among themselves, there is, by and large, no conflict, no sin, no disobedience, and no theft in Elephant. A passerby left a large sum of money in Elephant's godhouse. When he returned the next day, the money was still lying on the floor where he had left it.

The Elephant kinship system differs only slightly from that of Gopalpur, but Elephant bears a peculiar cross. During the dry season, there is no water. Drinking water must be brought from the valley, five hundred feet below. When it comes to marriage, few fathers wish to give their daughters to Elephant. To make their village more attractive, men make special concessions to their wives, such as carrying water and fetching wood. Wives are treated with the greatest circumspection, for should one leave, it would not be easy to find another. Men take care, when there is a divorce, to see that the wife marries another man from Elephant. Many men have had two or three wives and in some cases, appear to have exchanged wives.

There are only Leatherworkers and Lingayats in Elephant, its Stoneworkers, Blacksmiths, Carpenters, and Barbers coming from other villages. The Washerman is a member of the Lingayat jati, as is the Priest. To people in Elephant, the major significance of jati is that their own is superior to all others.

An Urban Village

Sixty miles north of Elephant and some three hundred miles south of Gopalpur, stands the village of Namhalli. Namhalli is roughly the same size as Gopalpur and, like it, is a village of middle-class, small farmers belonging to a number of different jatis. The major difference between Namhalli and the villages of Elephant and Gopalpur is that Namhalli possesses a history. In Elephant and Gopalpur, the oldest of old men are able to remember only a few changes, and those concern mainly births, marriages, and deaths. In Namhalli, even a young man can list hundreds of changes that have occurred during his lifetime. Namhalli stands only a half hour's bus ride away from the modern industrial city of Bangalore. Gopalpur and Elephant participate in regional cultures that are from time to time subjected to pressures from the outside world; for Namhalli, there is no longer an outside world.

Namhalli, like Gopalpur, is located on a plain and contains many kinds of land within its limits. At its lower end is a small stream surrounded by rice lands. Nearer is a canal used to irrigate the small gardens, that line its banks. The village itself is located in the center of a three-hundred acre patch of dry, unirrigated land used for the growing of red millet. The houses are made of mud brick, and the roofs are covered with machine-made interlocking tile. The walls are whitewashed inside and out; the floors are covered with cement or a plaster of cow dung. Many of the houses resemble the urban bungalows found in the nearby city. There are, generally, two or three rooms, including a room near the entrance where cattle are kept and agricultural equipment is stored. Agricultural equipment is essentially similar to that used in Gopalpur, except that every farmer owns an iron plow.

Women in Namhalli dress very much like the women of Gopalpur and Elephant, but their saris are of lighter material and are usually machine-made. Men dress like the men of Bangalore. Many own suits of European cut for special occasions. Even more own long trousers, which they wear with shoes and socks whenever they leave the village. Inside the village, most people wear short trousers, shirts, and a towel thrown carelessly over the right shoulder. Although the men of Gopalpur and Elephant frequently wear sandals, when working, men in Namhalli work barefoot, wearing footgear on special occasions. The sandals worn in Namhalli are machine-made and disintegrate rapidly if used elsewhere than on city streets. In the evening, men frequently tie a wrap-around dhoti over their trousers and cover themselves in soft, machine-made blankets. Namhalli is more than four thousand feet above sea level and it is never warm after dark.

The economic life is infinitely more complex than that of Gopalpur, for Namhalli, over the past twenty years, has made the transition from rural village to quasi-suburb. Namhalli continues to raise red millet and cattle fodder for its internal consumption, but many other crops are grown for sale and consumption in the city. Almost every year a new crop is introduced, and in its gardens are produced coconuts, ginger, tomatoes, potatoes, cabbage, cauliflower, sweet potatoes, chilies, eggplant, coffee, tobacco, oranges, mangoes, limes, gourds, betel leaf, areca nut, grapes, cucumbers, canteloupe, radishes, and more besides. Because the city is desperately hungry for fruit and "European vegetables," the profit to be derived from their production rises every year. The government controls the price of grain, but it has never been able to control the price of fresh fruits and vegetables.

One acre planted to potatoes in 1960 produced two truckloads full. Abdul, the planter, estimates that the cost of producing the potatoes, including his own labor and the manure produced by his own cattle, was Rs. 714, the equivalent of two year's wages for an unskilled day worker, or about $143. The two truckloads were sold for Rs. 1920, a net profit of Rs. 1206. The large yield was made possible by the purchase of seed potatoes and the use of chemical manure and insecticide. If a Muslim graduate of the local junior high school can make that kind of profit from one acre, a Shepherd, graduated from the same school, plans to do even better. Malla has devoted an acre of garden to the growing of grapes. Grapevines yield twice a year near Bangalore and, after four years, Malla hopes to receive an annual net profit of three thousand rupees, about equal to his initial investment. With very little outside help, the people of Namhalli and its region have devised a means of producing fantastic profits from tiny patches of land.

But Namhalli, located near the city, has enjoyed the benefits of modern medical and public health practices for many years. Its population has increased to a point where there are only about three acres of land per family in the village, yet it suffers a desperate shortage of labor. So severe is this that many men have planted productive lands to Casuarina trees, which will be used for firewood. They produce a reasonable profit after ten years, and require no labor beyond the initial planting. The shortage of labor stems from the fact that a great many people are school teachers, factory laborers, and minor government officials. Namhalli's success in obtaining these government jobs reflect the emphasis that parents have placed on education.

Children in Gopalpur tend to run wild receiving little formal training. In Elephant, they are trained to sit for long hours memorizing traditional materials, and in Namhalli to be noisy, mischievous, curious, and alert. Akkayamma describes her child:

My daughter came home from school at eleven o'clock. I told her to get some firewood. She said, "I am frightened, I won't go." I hit her five or six times. She went off crying and brought some fire wood. I served her some food and she ate. She went out to play. A blind boy was standing in the street, she recited, "Tie the blind one to a stick, tie the blind one to a tree, dance like a blind man." I gave my daughter a good beating and she cried. The school bell rang, my daughter washed her hands and feet. Then she ate and went to school. On the way home from school she teased a lame boy. The lame boy told me. I took a stick and beat her thoroughly.

She went out to play with some boys. They were playing, "Man Keeps Sand Heaps." In this game, all the children make heaps of dirt and whoever makes the fewest heaps is beaten. Whenever the other children weren't looking, my daughter stole their sand heaps. Because she had the most heaps, my daughter was able to beat the other children. After a while, they realized that she was stealing their heaps and calculated that she was fifty sand heaps short. They all hit her fifty times. When my daughter reported this to me, I said, "Why did you eat all of those blows!" I hit her two or three times. After that she helped me grind some grain and I sang her some nuptial wedding songs such as "Borrow for the wedding, make holes in the house." Then I told her some riddles such as, "It sews but it isn't a needle, it turns, but it isn't a wheel, it talks but it isn't a man."

After eating we both slept. In the morning, she went to school, but she left that at nine o'clock and came home. "I am hungry," she said. I fed her and she went back to school. When she came home at eleven, I said, "What did the Master tell you today?" "He taught us a song, 'Oh, yellow one, spread your yellow head quickly; oh, shining one, balance your head, cobra. I will play the flute, listen to the tune—ta, ta, ta, ta, ta, ta.' "

Akkayamma's daughter is nearly six years old and will soon begin to receive regular instruction from the school master. In the meantime, Akkayamma's daughter and other children old enough to walk will attend the school from time to time. The regularly enrolled school child is grilled by both parents when he comes home from school. The interest is not casual, father and son sit side by side for an hour or more going over the school day in detail. When night falls, the scholar sits under the single electric light bulb and goes over his lessons. Mothers beat their children, but they also boast at length concerning their clever pranks. Almost everyone in Namhalli is literate, and most of the young men are high school graduates. Namhalli's concern with education and with children probably reflects the fact that the parent regards the child as an agent of his own social mobility, a person who will lead him out of the farmer class into the "educated class."

In 1953, Namhalli possessed only one high school graduate and only a few people who held salaried jobs. Many were hungry, and mothers were beginning to practice infanticide and abortion in order to dispose of unwanted children. Jobs in agriculture and in the city were hard to find. The village seemed to lack any sense of direction or purpose. The old patterns of relationship between kinsmen and among the jatis no longer seemed effective. Conflict among brothers, between husband and wife, between different jatis, even between friends, seemed to be endemic. Almost every day there was a suicide, a wife beating, a theft, or a violent quarrel. The traditional village organization, a Headman, an Accountant, and a council of representatives from each of the jatis in the village, seemed unable to cope with the existing pattern of conflict. Necessary cooperation to maintain water courses within the village, to repair village streets and approach roads, to purify drinking water wells, and to carry on the social and ceremonial life of the village, was not forthcoming.

Between 1953 and 1960, however, factories in Bangalore were enlarged and several new ones were built. A demand was created for skilled and semi-skilled laborers who were literate and who could speak English. Namhalli established a relationship with a particular factory, and now, every morning and afternoon, buses come from the factory to collect salaried employees who will spend the day operating complex machinery in factories that are as modern as any in the world.

The practical approach to life, characteristic of the traditional cultures of both Gopalpur and Namhalli, led people in Namhalli to reject their old ways when they saw the benefits of a city job, and to accept, almost overnight, "modern" ways of doing things. Workers from Namhalli learned not only new ways of doing things in the factory, but also new ways of organizing the village. Formerly, nothing could be accomplished unless the heads of every family in the village unanimously agreed to do it. Now, if something is to be done, those who feel like doing so contribute to the establishment of a "chit fund." Every month, the sum collected is auctioned to the highest bidder who uses it for a month, and returns it together with the interest he originally agreed to pay. In this way, the farmer obtains operating capital necessary to purchase improved seed or chemical manure. When the chit fund is large enough to pay for a bus trip for the village school children, or to rebuild the village godhouse, or to complete whatever project it was established for, the money is used for that purpose.

As a member of the labor union at the factory, the laborer has access to political power. Where government officials hover on the outskirts of Gopalpur and try to force people to adopt more modern ways, government officials enter Namhalli by request. To the people of Gopalpur, government officials are persons to be feared and appeased. To the people of Namhalli, government officials are public servants, "just like ourselves." In the year 1953, a group of men complained to the police concerning the activities of some of their neighbors, the first time anyone in Namhalli had ever approached the police voluntarily. When the police came, they threatened and browbeat the villagers and collected handsome bribes. Now, when a policeman visits, the leaders of the village chat with him as if he were an old friend. If he threatened anyone or tried to collect bribes, he would be reported, and officials of the factory and the labor union would complain to the higher-ranking police officials.

The commitment to modern ways reaches deep into Namhalli. Every month, the factory laborer carefully peruses the company magazine, and scrupulously follows the advice contained in articles dealing with nutrition, child raising, and the proper way to brush one's teeth. Each of the factory laborers subscribes to a journal or newspaper. After he reads it, it is filed in the village library. People read everything, the *Daily Worker, Screen,* the *Times of India.*

Although many people have adopted modern ways, it is worth noting that the traditional way of life has not been forgotten, nor is it dead. It has been reworked, reformulated, and enriched. Many no longer believe in the relative superiority or inferiority of jatis, so that men in different jatis eat together, and almost everyone has tasted beef. Even the restrictions against associating with members of the Leatherworker jati seem to continue only in deference to the feelings of the aged. Although young men, influenced by the cinema, believe in romantic love and frown on arranged marriages, they somehow do not fall in love with women from other jatis. The Barber carries on his business in a neighboring larger village in a modern shop; the Washerman operates a laundry near one of the factories; the Blacksmith works in a factory making things out of metal; the Weaver works in a textile mill. Not all factory employment follows jati lines, however, and men of many different jatis work in factories. One of the Blacksmiths came home from the factory one day and said:

Every day I eat lunch with a Christian and a Brahmin. Today, the Brahmin looked into the Christian's lunch pail and saw a piece of something there. The Brahmin said, "What's that?" The Christian said, "You wouldn't be interested in that." The Brahmin said, "Come on, let me have a piece of it." The Christian said, "No, you shouldn't be eating that." The Brahmin reached into the Christian's lunch pail and took that stuff and ate it.

Almost certainly, the Brahmin had previously consumed beef in secret, probably as a daring youthful escapade. To consume beef publicly, without fear of consequences, is another matter.

But it is not just the influence of the city that distinguishes Namhalli from Gopalpur. There are striking differences between the older traditions of the two villages. Marriage ceremonies in Namhalli seem never to have been as elaborate as those of Gopalpur. Although a bride price is paid, it has always been a trivial sum. While women are supposed to begin to sleep with their husbands immediately after puberty, Namhalli has always considered puberty to begin at the age of sixteen. As in Gopalpur, marriages in Namhalli have always been considered to represent the establishment of linkages between two villages, but Namhalli's circle of related villages is far larger than that of Gopalpur, and many marriages create connections as far as forty miles away. Lineages in Gopalpur are short and rarely extend beyond two or three villages. In Namhalli, there is a regular lineage organization; all members of one lineage worship the same "house god," and come together periodically at a temple dedicated to him. Thousands of people may have the same house god and belong to the same lineage. The lineage organization has a council of elders and a religious leader who keeps a record of lineage membership and must be consulted when a marriage is being planned. In modern times, it is not clear whether such consultations occur, or whether the religious leaders still maintain records.

Just as the marriage circle in Namhalli is broadened by the formal keeping of records, so the size of jatis is enlarged by the development of formal jati organizations. Jatis, as well, have their councils of elders, and religious leaders, who consult their records to determine whether or not a particular individual is a member of the jati. There is also a mechanism for expelling persons from the jati. Jatis are linked together in interjati organizations called the "bundle of eighteen" and the "bundle of nine." Little is remembered concerning the functioning of these organizations, but it is known that the two organizations are in conflict, and that one's own is higher than the other. Although for practical reasons jatis agree to accept an order of ranking on particular occasions, there is no consistent and generally agreed upon ranking of jatis. Lingayats claim to be superior to Brahmins, and Blacksmith–Carpenters claim to be superior to either Brahmins or Lingayats.

The Gopalpur region, the Elephant region, and the Namhalli region are different facets of the civilization of Mysore State. The people in each of them speak different dialects of the same language. The villages in all three are similar, but not identical. The school teacher of Namhalli sits on his veranda reading the financial section of an English language newspaper and notes the price of cotton in New York with keen satisfaction. The cowherd in Elephant follows his animals through the forest. He wears sandals and a strip of cloth six inches wide and, in 1953, was unaware that he was no longer a subject of the East India Company. All of these men, in Gopalpur, Elephant, and Namhalli, belong to the same culture. They all recognize the significance of jati, they all believe that it is sinful to disobey one's older brother, and they all hope to marry their sister's daughter.

Within the civilization of Mysore State, each village is the outcome of a unique compromise between its unique environment and the unique historical events that gave it birth and now maintain it. It is the task of the anthropologist to describe and explain those uniquely separate, yet strangely interlinked, entities called cultures and civilizations.

Recommended Reading

DUBE, S. C. *Indian Village*. Ithaca, N.Y.: Cornell University Press, 1955.

A straightforward description of a village located ninety miles east of Gopalpur, near the city of Hyderabad.

LEWIS, OSCAR, *Village Life in Northern India*. Illinois: University of Illinois Press, 1958.

A village located far from Gopalpur in a densely populated region where patterns of marriage and of daily life are quite different. Presents a relatively extended discussion of political life and conflict within the village.

MARRIOTT, MCKIM (Ed.), *Village India*. Chicago: University of Chicago Press, 1955.

A series of descriptions of villages in various parts of India. Each village is discussed from a particular viewpoint.

MAYER, ADRIAN, *Caste and Kinship in Central India*. Berkeley and Los Angeles: University of California Press, 1960.

The finest study yet published of the workings of caste and kinship in a single village and its region. The village resembles Gopalpur in some ways, and the villages of North India in others.

NARAYAN, R. K., *The Bachelor of Arts*. East Lansing, Michigan: Michigan State College Press, 1954.

First published in 1937, this novel is one of a series concerning the imaginary town of Malgudi in South India. Most novels about villages in India present drippingly sentimental accounts of conditions which are bad to begin with and then get worse. The novels of R. K. Narayan deal with real people in a manner sometimes critical, but always affectionate.

SRINIVAS, M. N. (Ed.), *India's Villages*. Bombay: Asia Publishing House, 1960.

These papers are descriptions of villages, first published in a Bombay magazine. Most of the papers were written while the authors were in the field.

VON FURER-HAIMENDORF, CHRISTOPH AND ELIZABETH, *The Reddis of the Bison Hills*. London: Macmillan, 1945.

The Reddis are a tribal people who speak Telegu, a language familiar to many people in Gopalpur. Their way of life, presented here with loving detail, provides interesting contrasts with that of Gopalpur.

WISER, CHARLOTTE VIALL AND WILLIAM H. *Behind Mud Walls*. New York: Richard R. Smith, 1930.

A North Indian village described by sociologically trained missionaries. This is the first detailed description of an Indian village by persons with scientific training.

Glossary

BHAJANE: Religious songs or hymns, the night long ceremony where a god is worshipped and the men sing until a ceremonial meal, prepared by the women, is ready.

CHEETA: A leopard with black spots fond of goats, sheep, and calves.

GHI: Clarified butter, one of the ritually pure substances produced by the cow.

GAUDA: A prosperous landowner, frequently the headman of a village.

JATI: Literally, a race or breed of men, used to refer to the identifiable groupings or "castes" within the region. Jatis are ordinarily ranked, usually endogamous, and sometimes possess unique occupational, religious or cultural characteristics.

JATRA: A festival in which one village entertains neighboring villages. It involves religious ritual, games, performances, feasting and commercial activity.

KALI YUGA: The Age of Kali, a time of divine misrule during which the affairs of the ordinary world are in a state of confusion and immorality.

MAVLA: A Muslim priest, the priestly jati within the Muslim jati.

NIM: A tree, *Azadirachta indica,* valued for its shade, aroma, timber, and medical and religious efficacy.

RUPEE: A coin worth twenty-one cents in foreign exchange, but worth more than a dollar in terms of its value in purchasing locally made goods. It will buy a lavish meal in the best hotel in Yadgiri, a good quality undershirt or a bottle of brandy.

SAMSARA: Family life, the confused picture of reality transmitted by the six senses of sight, hearing, touch, taste, smell and pain.

TAHSILDAR: The administrative officer in charge of a region containing three hundred to six hundred villages.